Francis Thompson

Twayne's English Authors Series

Herbert Sussman, Editor

Northeastern University

TEAS 436

FRANCIS THOMPSON
(1859–1907)
Portrait painted by John Lavalle
Photograph courtesy of the Special Collections,
Boston College Library

Francis Thompson

By Beverly Taylor

University of North Carolina at Chapel Hill

Twayne Publishers
A Division of G.K. Hall & Co. • Boston

Francis Thompson

Beverly Taylor

Copyright © 1987 by G.K. Hall & Co.
All Rights Reserved
Published by Twayne Publishers
A Division of G.K. Hall & Co.
70 Lincoln Street
Boston, Massachusetts 02111

Copyediting supervised by Lewis DeSimone
Book production by Elizabeth Todesco
Book design by Barbara Anderson

Typeset in 11 pt. Garamond
by P&M Typesetting, Inc., Waterbury, Connecticut

Printed on permanent/durable acid-free paper
and bound in the United States of America

Library of Congress Cataloging in Publication Data

Taylor, Beverly.
    Francis Thompson.

    (Twayne's English authors series ; TEAS 436)
    Bibliography: p. 149
    Includes index.
    1. Thompson, Francis, 1859–1907—Criticism and interpretation.
I. Title. II. Series.
PR5651.T39   1987   821'.8   86-14928
ISBN 0-8057-6930-7

Contents

About the Author

Beverly Taylor, Associate Professor of English at the University of North Carolina at Chapel Hill, was graduated from the University of Mississippi and received M.A. and Ph.D. degrees from Duke University. She has collaborated on *The Return of King Arthur: British and American Arthurian Literature Since 1800* and on *Arthurian Legend and Literature* (2 volumes). She has coedited a collection of essays, *The Cast of Consciousness: Concepts of the Mind in British and American Romanticism,* and has published articles on Byron, Shelley, Tennyson, Browning, Arnold, and Carlyle, as well as Chaucer and Gottfried von Strassburg. She is currently editing the complete poetry of Francis Thompson and compiling an anthology of his criticism.

Preface

Describing Francis Thompson in *The Victorian Age in Literature,* G. K. Chesterton observed that "perhaps the shortest definition of the Victorian Age is that he stood outside it." His stylistic eccentricities, especially his ingenious metaphors and verbal ornamentation, led his contemporaries to link him with seventeenth-century Metaphysical poets such as Crashaw. He stood apart from the Aesthetes and Decadents of his day in his subject matter and themes, and differed from the poets of the so-called Catholic literary revival in his style. Today known primarily for only one poem, the splendid ode "The Hound of Heaven," Thompson, whose publishing career lasted from 1888 to 1907, is generally thought to stand outside the twentieth century as well.

Even before his death his poetry remained very much the province of Catholic editors and readers, and twentieth-century editions and studies of his work have done little to expand his audience. Some readers have been attracted by the story of his life, by the incongruity of a drug-addicted vagrant penning the soaring, mystical verse for which he is known. But neither the religious nor the biographical interest suggests Thompson's true range or artistic stature.

Besides the religious poems richly imbued with the symbolism and theology of Catholicism but readily accessible to a non-Catholic audience, Thompson's canon of approximately three hundred poems includes many works more to the taste of twentieth-century readers. The modern appeal of Thompson's art has been obscured by the unavailability of a large proportion of his poetry. In addition to the elaborate and rhapsodic verse with which he is identified, he wrote satiric, ironic, and comic poems, often in a spare, colloquial style. Whatever his tone or subject, Thompson loaded his work with imagery that has rarely been surpassed in resourcefulness, power, or abundance. Although most studies of his works have focused on their religious or biographical significance, Thompson's poems deserve attention for their artistic proficiency and technical experimentation. Many pieces that have been viewed as interesting biographical documents but inferior poetry may more properly be considered consciously crafted artistic exercises.

FRANCIS THOMPSON

In addition to his poetry, Thompson wrote more than 450 reviews and essays, most of them published anonymously and almost entirely neglected today. This prose commands interest not only for the full picture it gives of late nineteenth-century literary taste, or for the consistently stimulating analyses of individual writers, but also for Thompson's flexible metaphoric style, which enlivens even the driest subjects.

The purpose of this study is to introduce the neglected Thompson, suggesting the quality of the conscious c.aftsman who has remained obscured by the Catholic apologist and the imagined bohemian. Chapter 1 discusses his biography, stripped of the myths that during his life and immediately following his death camouflaged the less romantic actualities. Chapters 2 and 3 analyze the three volumes of poetry published in his lifetime. Attention to the themes and patterns in the two collections of poems reveals a level of careful crafting not previously noted in his works. Chapter 4 surveys the large body of poetry that was uncollected in Thompson's lifetime, much of which remains little known and even unpublished today. The final chapter surveys the prose, especially focusing on Thompson's literary theory and critical judgments that enhance our understanding of his own poetic practice.

As any student of Thompson must be, I am deeply indebted to the late Reverend Terence L. Connolly, whose work has made available most of the prose now attributed to Thompson, as well as important bibliographies, catalogs of manuscript materials, and editions of previously unprinted poetry. John Walsh's biography of Thompson, *Strange Harp, Strange Symphony,* has provided significant facts previously undisclosed, as well as fresh interpretations of known data.

I am grateful to the trustees of the Wilfrid Meynell estate for their permission to publish manuscript materials and to Boston College for access to their invaluable Thompson Collection. My work with these manuscripts has been facilitated by grants from the Research Council of the University of North Carolina at Chapel Hill, the American Council of Learned Societies, the American Philosophical Society, and the National Endowment for the Humanities. I am also indebted to Edmund Reiss for generous encouragement, advice, and criticism.

Beverly Taylor

*University of North Carolina
at Chapel Hill*

Chronology

1859 Born 18 December in Preston, Lancashire, the son of Charles Thompson, a physician, and Mary Morton Thompson, both Catholic converts.

1864 Family moves to Ashton-under-Lyne, near Manchester.

1870 Enters St. Cuthbert's College, Ushaw, a Catholic school in Durham.

1877 Enrolls at Owens Medical College, Manchester, where for six years he unsuccessfully studies medicine.

1879 Probably begins using laudanum.

1880 His mother dies on 19 December.

1885 Leaves home, 8 November, for three years of vagrancy in London.

1887 February, mails to the editor Wilfrid Meynell an essay and some poems. Summer, an unnamed prostitute befriends him.

1888 Spring, attempts suicide. April, his first poem appears in *Merry England*. May, meets Wilfrid Meynell.

1889 Recuperates from drug withdrawal at a monastery in Storrington, Sussex. Writes "The Hound of Heaven."

1890 March, returns to London. Contributes to the Meynells' two periodicals. Summer and fall, composes *Sister Songs*.

1892 December, takes up residence at a monastery in Pantasaph, Wales, after relapsing into drug addiction.

1893 Begins an uneasy love affair with Maggie Brien, who inspires *A Narrow Vessel*. December, publishes his first collection, *Poems*.

1894 October, begins important friendship with Coventry Patmore which lasts until Patmore's death in November 1896.

1895 June, publishes *Sister Songs*.

1896 Summer, visits London and begins relationship with Katie King, who inspires many lyrics. December, returns to London, beginning a campaign to support himself by journalism and win Katie.

1897   May, publishes *New Poems*.

1900   Abandons plan to publish another collection of poetry; resumes steady use of laudanum.

1906   Boards at a monastery in Crawley, Sussex.

1907   Dies in a London hospital, 13 November, of tuberculosis and "morphomania."

Chapter One

Beyond the Ways
of "Comfortable Men"

Two years before his death Francis Thompson wrote, "In my youth I sighed against monotony, & wanted romance; now I dread romance. Romance is romantic only for the hearers & onlookers, not for the actors. . . . Once step aside from the ways of 'comfortable men,' you cannot regain them. You will live & die under the law of the intolerable thing they call romance."[1] Ranging between monotony and near tragedy, most of Thompson's adult life would probably seem devoid of romance to observers, yet from his twenty-fifth year, when he drifted in London as a drug-addicted derelict, he in a real sense cut himself off from the ways of "comfortable men." He was to control his addiction during much of the time remaining in his life and to achieve fame as a poet as well as fairly steady employment as a contributor to periodicals. He was also to measure out his days in largely prosaic, repetitious conversations and unvaried activities, but he was never to escape the law of "the intolerable thing they call romance" dictated by his eccentric nature.

A stone tablet and a bronze plaque marking Francis Joseph Thompson's birthplace bear two different birthdates. This conflict fittingly introduces an account of his life, for the faces he presented to the world were consistently contradictory and ambiguous. As a poet he was vital, sensitive, and sophisticated; as a man, often slothful, irresponsible, and childish. He aspired to the responsibilities of the priesthood but proved incapable of ordering his own existence. In critical prose he cannily assessed what constitutes good verse, while he sometimes betrayed these principles in his own poetry. With some, he was a fascinating, even perhaps profound, thinker and talker—"full of the best talk"—while to others he was notoriously repetitious and mundane.[2] His period of dereliction in London is largely a blank, known to us only from fragmentary recollections that Thompson sketched in conversations and in scant poetic allusions. Although the later years are more fully recorded, behind the facts of dates and events the man himself often remains hidden, probably intentionally so. As Thompson noted, he early in life became "expert in concealment, not expression, of myself. Expression I reserved for my pen. My tongue was tenaciously disciplined in silence."[3] Often when he did allow his pen to reveal the man, he quickly abbreviated the exposure. After writing that he had sacrificed the ways of "comfortable men," for example, he checked his lament: "But I never meant to write all this."[4] What facts are known in his biography compel one to regard his literary achievement, in the face of an erratic and disturbing life, as truly remarkable.

Youth

Though the bronze plaque affixed in 1926 to Thompson's birthplace at 7 Winckley Street in Preston, Lancashire, commemorates his birthdate as 16 December 1859, as the stone tablet records, he was probably born on 18 December.[5] Confusion over the day is less surprising than Thompson's own uncertainty about the year: "I was born in 1858 or 1859 (I never could remember and don't care which)."[6] Similarly faulty recollection or unconcern with time was to bedevil his social and professional life. Yet he grew up in a well-regulated household, in a family that followed the ways of "comfortable men" and was, moreover, essentially congenial and sympathetic. Most important, the home was steeped in Catholic piety. His father, Charles Thompson, shared the zeal of a family in which both his parents and four of his siblings converted to Catholicism. The religious intensity of the poet's mother, Mary Morton, was doubtless reinforced by the opposition of her Anglican family, who for a time turned her out of the house because of her religious conversion. Before her marriage in 1857 she had briefly entered religious retreat at a convent, but went on to become a governess. Her daughter Mary, the elder of the poet's two surviving sisters, subsequently became a nun.

From 1864, when Francis was five, Charles Thompson conducted his medical practice in their new home, Ashton-under-Lyne, an industrial suburb of Manchester. Unsympathetic attitudes toward Catholicism limited the family to a very small, though close circle of friends among fellow Catholics, especially the priests in the area. As an altar boy, Francis perhaps exhibited greater interest in a colorful cassock than in the symbolic functions of his office, but he always loved church ritual, which he once called "poetry addressed to the eye."[7] This Catholic upbringing underlies much of the content, language, and imagery of his works and planted the seed for some of the most evocative mystical poetry in the English language.

Previous biographies may have overemphasized the solitary nature of young Francis as an introverted boy sitting on the household stairway, isolated within his world of books. Recollections of family and acquaintances attest "Frank's" inclination to lively pranks and fairly typical boyhood fellowship.[8] His most frequent companions were his two younger sisters, Mary and Margaret, whom he entertained with imaginative diversions such as military assaults, card and magic tricks, and marionette performances in a small cardboard theater.[9] Yet Francis was essentially withdrawn, even in the midst of camaraderie: "My sport was solitary sport, even when I played with my sisters . . . my side of the game was part of a dream-scheme invisible to them." His sisters frequently chided this dreaming, exclaiming that Francis was "up in the moon again!"[10] His imaginative trips to the moon were on the whole more satisfying than his first trip to boarding school, when rowdier boys on the train crushed the bag of jam tarts that were to make his journey away from home somewhat palatable.

Shortly before his eleventh birthday in 1870 Francis entered the Catholic school of St. Cuthbert's, Ushaw College, in Durham. Not physically hardy, he nonetheless played handball and organized a pirate band inspired by his reading of adventure tales by Frederick Marryat and James Fenimore Cooper. In later years he magnified the frustrations and embarrassments of his school days. Long after being initiated by a paddling in front of laughing schoolmates, Thompson castigated the "malignity of my tormentors . . . more lacerating than the pain itself. It seemed to me—virginal to the world's ferocity—a hideous thing that strangers should dislike me, should delight and triumph in pain to me, though I had done them no ill and bore them no malice." To him the schoolboys were "devilish apparitions" and "testimonies to the murky aboriginal demon in man."[11] Thompson projected his own sensitivity to the coarseness of childish sensibilities and the cruel aspects of life at boarding school in his "Essay on Shelley," where in a long, scathing passage he imagines Shelley's reaction against schoolboy tormentors similar to his own. But in later life Thompson tended to overdramatize his misfortunes, and the bitterness of his recollections does not correspond with those of his colleagues and teachers, who recalled his school days as not exuberant, but at least not morbid or painful.

At any rate, his equanimity was sufficient for him to succeed in his studies. He excelled in English, Latin, and Greek. Of twenty-one competitive exams held in essay writing during his seminary days, he won first place in sixteen; he was usually first in English and often first or second in Latin. He also fell to last place in mathematics.[12] (This last signal should have been better heeded later when Thompson left Ushaw and entered medical college by virtue of winning distinction in Greek on the entrance examination, only to fail, after six years, to attain competence in the scientific course of study.) At Ushaw as at home, Francis lived most fully in an imaginative world stimulated by literature. To his established list of favorites—William Shakespeare, Walter Scott, Thomas Babington Macaulay, Samuel Taylor Coleridge, and Percy Bysshe Shelley—he added Edmund Spenser, Richard Crashaw, and other seventeenth-century Metaphysical poets who would extensively influence his poetry.

His growing interest in literature probably contributed to his failure in pursuing the priesthood. Though he had wished from boyhood to become a priest and at Ushaw had formally declared his intention to take Holy Orders, by age seventeen he had become "devoured with literary ambition."[13] He was always highly affected by church ritual and Marian worship, but at this time he did not evince particular piety or interest in theology.[14] Finally school authorities advised Dr. Thompson that Francis was unsuited to the priesthood for two principal reasons—his "strong, nervous timidity" and (even more telling) "a natural *indolence*."[15] In truth, indolence rather than ambition to write poetry seems to have impeded his first career plans, for once freed from his commitment to the priesthood, Francis did not hasten to achieve his poetic aspirations.

He had composed a few verses during his days at Ushaw, nine of which survive in a school notebook. They reflect his boyish interests in combat and adventure, as well as a delight in satire and humor that throughout his life prompted jottings of doggerel, penned even in times of great despair. Derivative verses on nature and love reveal the influence of Shelley, Wordsworth, and Keats.[16] The only hint of Thompson's mature style is the predilection for archaic words and spellings that remained so pronounced in his poetry. None of the schoolboy verses signals the earnest beginning of a career or even a major preoccupation. Over the next six years Thompson, relatively indolent as his schoolmasters warned, produced little verse (some twenty poems may be assigned to this period)—and little else.

Shortly before his eighteenth birthday, having left Ushaw without taking Holy Orders, he enrolled in Owens Medical College in Manchester, with no apparent reason besides the example of his father's career, the proximity of the school, and his father's natural desire that the boy do something. Thompson much later explained to a friend that he could never stand the sight of flowing blood, but for six years he successfully maintained the illusion that he was studying for the profession.[17] At the end of his second year he took the medical examinations in London, failed, repeated the attempt in 1881 and again in 1884—this time in Glasgow, where the standards were thought to be less stringent. Presumably Francis fulfilled the minimal requirements at Owens, for Dr. Thompson never received notice of excessive absence; however, the reluctant student spent as much time as possible in the libraries, museums, and art galleries of Manchester. All the while he never said a word to suggest that he found medical study uncongenial, even though both he and his sister indicated that Dr. Thompson would have relented if he had understood his son's feelings.[18] Many years of estrangement later, when Dr. Thompson heard of Francis's newly acquired fame as a poet, he exclaimed, "If the lad had but told me!"[19] The father might well have had an answer to his son's notebook musing, "What does one want with a tongue when one has silence?"[20]

But the natural indolence that Ushaw authorities noted cannot finally be blamed for the years of unproductivity following 1877, for during that time—probably in 1879—Francis fell into the unnatural sloth induced by laudanum. The familiar cases of Coleridge and Thomas De Quincey remind us that this preparation, a tincture of opium in alcohol, was the most frequently used mild painkiller in an age when medical science understood very little about addiction. The drug was easily obtained at pharmacies without prescription. Manchester was particularly noted for the widespread use of laudanum among textile factory workers. The drug was, moreover, available to Francis at home in Dr. Thompson's medical offices and at Owens College facilities.

Besides the availability of the drug, an exciting stimulus may have prompted this introverted, purposeless youth of literary inclinations to sample the effects of laudanum. Probably in 1879, Francis received from his mother a gift that accrued additional significance because she died not long after presenting it—De Quincey's *Confessions of an English Opium Eater.* Even before receiving his mother's gift copy, Thompson had apparently been much affected by the powerful visionary qualities of the work and had talked about it so much that his uncle recalled it as Francis's favorite book, adding the puzzling remark, "We had often said his experiences would surpass those of De Quincey."[21] Even though the *Confessions* illustrates the horrors of opium addiction, it also appears to describe blessings, especially in the dream sequences, that must have appealed to the youth who preferred being "up in the moon" to pursuing an uncongenial career in a rather ugly industrial community. Thompson later identified De Quincey's dream narratives as "the crowning glory" of the book— "passages of such vaporous sublimity . . . , such ministerial grandeurs of style, as we know not where else to look for."[22] That this visionary author, who had also lived in Manchester, had begun using opium at about the same age as his enthusiastic reader must have suggested to Francis the flattering and dangerous possibility of similarities between them. In fact, Thompson came to regard De Quincey with the feeling of "a younger for an elder brother," and throughout his life he emulated De Quincey in various ways.[23] He adopted the older writer's characteristic of writing "ȳ" for *the,* and more significantly, when he was finally to run away from home in 1885, he was to follow De Quincey's precedent of setting out with few possessions besides two prized volumes of English and classical poetry.[24] After months of wretched, degrading experiences even worse than De Quincey's early London days, Thompson would also receive aid from a prostitute whom he described in details so closely following De Quincey's narrative that life—or Thompson's imagination—would seem to have imitated art.

His drug addiction did not, of course, stem only from veneration of De Quincey. Friends and early biographers attributed his laudanum dependence to treatment for a serious illness in 1879, but no evidence confirms this justification, even though Thompson may well have been sick at this time.[25] Contributing factors other than illness and excitement over the *Confessions* certainly existed: pressure to find something to do after failing to enter the priesthood and, most especially, the death of his mother, unquestionably the most important person in his life. In addition, a major factor must have been Thompson's avowed reluctance to assume responsibility in the adult world: "I did not want to grow up; did not want emancipation from parental control, fine clothes, dissipation, freedom and worldly pleasures. I did not want responsibility, did not want to be a man. I did not much want even fame, and soon abandoned it as hopeless. . . . Toys I could surrender (with chagrin) so I had my great toy of the imagination, whereby the world became to me my box of toys."[26]

If the reasons for Thompson's addiction were not obvious, the results were. While he was still attending medical college, he frequently procured money for laudanum by requesting cash for school fees, and on occasion by pawning or selling equipment such as his microscope.[27] After failing the medical examinations for the third time, twenty-four-year-old Francis acceded to his father's demands that he get a job, working briefly for a manufacturer of medical instruments, then undertaking to sell an encyclopedia. Characteristically, he spent two months reading it, then abandoned it unsold. He also enlisted in the army, spent perhaps a month in drills that aimed to improve his physical stamina, only to be rejected—probably because of his addiction. A year and a half after Francis left medical school Dr. Thompson charged his listless son with either drinking or stealing laudanum from the medical supplies in his office.[28] This confrontation on 8 November 1885 finally goaded the youth into the "emancipation from parental control, . . . dissipation . . . and worldly pleasures" that he did not want. During that night Francis— a month short of turning twenty-six—left home for Manchester, planning like his revered De Quincey to travel to London.

Early Life in London

Thompson thus began nearly three years of dereliction in the city. Though he initially received a weekly allowance from his father and found a job collecting volumes for a bookshop, he soon forfeited the allowance by neglecting to collect it and exchanged regular employment for sporadic attempts to earn pennies in the streets. He held the reins of carriage horses, he ran behind vehicles to unload luggage, he sold matches, he blacked boots until policemen harried him from his corner. He at first delighted in the treasures of the Guildhall Library but soon became so shabby that he was barred from the building. Many nights he slept in a vagrants' shelter that provided mattresses in wooden boxes eerily resembling lidless coffins; other nights he slept in the open. Thompson's familiarity with poverty and degradation would have vitally charged a volume he later projected on the impressions of a wanderer in London's streets. He planned to depict "Fair London and Terrible London," but never completed the book— perhaps in part because he was too much acquainted with terrible London and too little with its fair counterpart.[29] His revulsion against the street life he had known is recorded in a letter from 1900: "These horrible streets, with their gangrenous multitudes, blackening ever into lower mortifications of humanity! The brute men; these lads who have almost lost the faculty of human speech, who howl & growl like animals, or use a tongue which is itself a cancerous disintegration of speech: these girls whose practice is a putrid ulceration of love. . . . The air is fulsome with its surcharge of tainted humanity."[30] His own experience with despair imparted special force to writings such as his review of General William Booth's *In Darkest England* (1891): "Misery cries out to me from the kerb-stone, despair passes me by in the ways; I discern limbs laden with fetters impalpable, but not imponderable; I hear the shaking of invisible lashes, I see men dabbled with their own oozing life."[31]

After nine months in the city Thompson briefly escaped poverty and homelessness through the charity of John McMaster, owner of a bootshop and a zealous Anglican. McMaster periodically rescued fallen brethren from the streets and restored them to respectability. He was later to describe the poet as his "only failure."[32] Thompson liked to recall that he had replied pertly to McMaster's surprising salutation—"Is your soul saved?"—by asserting his Catholic integrity: "What right have you to ask me that?"[33] This reply may be an apocryphal afterthought, but in any event McMaster proved adept at saving the body if not the soul. He saw to Thompson's physical needs for the next six months, while allowing the Catholic to confide his spiritual needs to the crucifix before which he prayed daily. McMaster also arranged for the runaway to rejoin the Thompson family in Ashton-under-Lyne for Christmas of 1886, but no reconciliation followed. By mid-January Thompson's laudanum addiction had become so extreme that he created problems in the bootshop, and his benefactor had to ask him to leave.

This respite, though temporary, permitted an important step toward securing more permanent rescue from the vagaries and deprivations of opium and the streets. While he was at McMaster's, Thompson wrote—even on old account books and scraps of paper. In 1886 the literary ambition that had seemed "consuming" in 1876 finally produced an essay, "Paganism Old and New," which was to return him—as near as was possible for Francis Thompson—to the ways of "comfortable men." The essay asserts that only with the flowering of Christianity did man achieve real poetic sensibility. Though the thesis might seem untenable, the essayist's performance is imposing. As one biographer has phrased Thompson's accomplishment, "this lonely, drug-captivated youth made casual allusion to Aeschylus, Sophocles, Homer, Cicero, Horace, Virgil, Tibullus, Catullus, Propertius, Ovid, Martial, Pliny, Statius, and Juvenal, . . . balanced quotations from Chaucer, Morris, Rossetti, Tennyson, Wordsworth, Shelley, Coleridge, De Quincey, and Collins, as well as some random remarks of Heine and Blake—all from memory. The style of the essay is pure, unhurried artistry."[34] Thompson also composed some verse at this time, including the "Dream-Tryst," which is his first notable poem. Enclosing a third piece—"The Passion of Mary," a brief poem written before he left home—he in February 1887 mailed his untidy manuscripts to Wilfrid Meynell, the editor of a Catholic literary monthly, *Merry England.* The cover letter betrays little expectation: "In enclosing the accompanying article for your inspection, I must ask pardon for the soiled state of the manuscript. It is due, not to slovenliness, but to the strange places and circumstances under which it has been written. . . . I enclose a stamped envelope for a reply; since I do not desire the return of the manuscript, regarding your judgment of its worthlessness as quite final." After signing "Yours with little hope," he added, "Kindly address your rejection to the Charing Cross Post Office."[35]

Meynell, an extremely busy editor, set the manuscript aside for about six months. When he finally read the essay, he tried unsuccessfully to reach its author. Thompson in the meantime had descended to the depths of poverty, addiction, and despair. He attempted suicide, but was interrupted by a timely apparition. As he later recounted the vision, Thomas Chatterton, the youthful poet who had taken his own life in London in the previous century, stopped Thompson just on the point of quaffing a lethal dose of laudanum. The legend that money arrived just a day too late to save Chatterton suggests that Thompson's vision embodied his hope of similar rescue. Aid arrived not only from this literary phantom but also from a prostitute who for some time shared her lodgings and income with the vagrant. His mixed feelings for the harlot—tenderness, gratitude, passion, revulsion—figure in several poems and a play fragment never published in his lifetime.[36] When Thompson later described this girl to friends, he depicted her as a gentle savior almost precisely fitting the mold of De Quincey's street girl Ann. When the opportunity of entering the respectable literary world confronted Thompson, he hesitated to leave the girl until she unselfishly broke their tie by disappearing. In the spring of 1888 Thompson discovered one of his poems in an issue of *Merry England,* for Meynell had printed it in hopes of drawing out the essayist of "Paganism Old and New." Thompson wrote Meynell, and the association which then began became the poet's lifeline for the rest of his existence. From the time he hesitatingly presented himself in the editor's office—clad in ragged clothes and broken shoes, with neither shirt nor socks—Meynell fed and clothed him, provided lodgings, medical care, and restorative respites out of London. Just as significantly, Meynell nurtured Thompson's literary talents, publishing his essays and poetry and arranging for him to contribute to other periodicals. Though only seven years older than the poet, Meynell in effect provided the parental control in mundane matters that Thompson had unwillingly forfeited, and became both his spiritual father in literary affairs and his most enthusiastic critic.

Essayist and Poet

Nearly thirty years old, Thompson finally began his literary career in earnest. After undergoing withdrawal from laudanum in a private hospital, he began to visit the Meynell household almost daily and to write reviews for *Merry England* and other periodicals. His prose, especially his essays on literary figures, was learned, provocative, and vigorous. Over subsequent years his contributions helped a great deal to establish the reputation of Meynell's journal. Despite his new activity, within six months Thompson had relapsed into drug addiction, and the editor arranged for him to move to a monastery at Storrington in Sussex. After experiencing the most devastating pangs of withdrawal and beginning a slow recovery, Thompson for the first time exhibited significant poetic talent. Before this he had shown Meynell some thirty-two poems that he considered his best work. Most were competent but undistinguished and imitative.[37] The first piece sent from Storrington, "Ode to the Setting Sun," developed out of the profound religious feeling of Thompson's youth and the richness of his immersion in literature. The ode delighted Meynell, who promptly featured it in *Merry England.* The poem opened the floodgates for a tide of verse over the next six months. The most important outcome of the year at Storrington was Thompson's beginning his most famous poem, "The Hound of Heaven," which records man's ambivalent resistance to the God he desires. The poem no doubt reflects the conflicting impulses of Thompson himself, so familiar with the ideal of grace and the reality of despair.

In March 1890 Thompson returned to London, longing for access to libraries and to greater intellectual stimulation than he found among country folk "sprung from the illicit union of a mowing machine and a turnip."[38] In addition to writing essays and verse for *Merry England,* he began participating in editorial work for a diocese newspaper also published by the Meynells, the *Weekly Register,* and contributing numerous articles under his own name and pseudonyms such as Francis Tancred, Francis Phillimore, and Philip Hemans.[39] His assistance in the frenzy to meet weekly deadlines was often more distracting than helpful, however, for he interrupted the intent group of workers with incessant trivia concerning his pens and ink and papers. Though he was little suited to the regimen of putting together a weekly paper, he was at this time—1890–1891—succeeding in his own creative endeavors. He wrote at least thirty serious poems, besides occasional verses for the papers, book reviews, and a lengthy study of St. John Baptist de la Salle, eighteenth-century founder of the Christian Brothers. He also composed the long work *Sister Songs,* an ornate tribute to Meynell's two young daughters and to the assistance the Meynell family had given him. In the spring of 1891 Thompson worked on a series of celebratory love poems that pay tribute to Wilfrid Meynell's wife.

Thompson's feelings for Alice Meynell are especially significant to both his life and his literary production. Most who met her considered her remarkable. She was an active journalist who not only wrote many articles for the Meynells' weekly and monthly publications but also shared the editorial responsibilities, all the while contributing essays to other journals. She was also a poet of increasing reputation, so well esteemed that when Tennyson died in 1892, she was considered a possible successor to the position of Poet Laureate. Thompson revered her talent and erudition: "I wonder what she does not know! A mistress of poetry, an exquisite art-critic, she knows, besides, music, Latin, Greek, Italian, French, German, and all kinds of multifarious things at which I can but dimly guess."[40] Although he usually resisted editors' interfering in his poetry, he took great pains to explain his intentions to her about any disputed point, and usually regarded her judgments as the final authority.[41] She was thus an important source of encouragement and critical guidance. In addition, as a counterpart to Wilfrid Meynell, she represented a mother figure who helped arrange the details of his life. Most important, she served Thompson's poetry as a symbol of mortal perfection that he associated with divine love.

In Alice Meynell, Thompson focused his long-established ideals of love and beauty. He had early in life revered the flawless beauty of dolls and of illustrations showing Shakespeare's heroines, and had determined that in living women, "beauty had expired somewhere about the time of Henry VIII" and love was not "a modern sentiment at all."[42] As a truant from medical school he had venerated a sculpture copied from the Vatican Melpomene: "each evening, . . . I stole to meditate and worship the baffling mysteries of her meaning. . . . Eyes of violet blue, drowsed-amorous, which surveyed me not, but looked ever beyond."[43] Thompson habitually idealized human love as a spiritual involvement analogous to divine love. On this impulse he often wrote to Alice Meynell as a remote, exalted being, much as troubadors addressed their ladies.[44] This reverential love for her underlies two series of poems, *Love in Dian's Lap* and a sequel, *Ultima.* Yet even in his most earnest worship of an ideal Thompson could see himself ironically. He once acknowledged to Alice Meynell, after declaring the spirituality of his regard, that "even a Seraph enamoured must be a trying guardian-angel to have to do with."[45] His idealizing treatment of love is closely related to his religious convictions, his love of ritual and symbol, and his devotion to the Virgin Mary; and most of his verses to Alice Meynell are cut from the same fabric as his religious and mystical verse.

Thompson was to have two less ethereal love relationships, besides his earlier liaison with the street girl—both were to be unfulfilling. The first budded during his second extended absence from London. In 1892 he had intensified his use of laudanum, to the point that the Meynells insisted he attempt further cure at the Franciscan monastery at Pantasaph. He went to the Welsh retreat in December and was to remain throughout most of the next four years. After the initial pain of withdrawal Thompson took some interest in Maggie Brien, the young daughter of his landlord. The association seems never to have developed very fully, but Thompson transformed the experience into a poetic sequence called *A Narrow Vessel,* which records the joys and disillusionment of love. Whatever the extent of personal reflections in the poems, Thompson insisted on their allegorical implications: "How many . . . have grasped the significance of my sequence, *A Narrow Vessel?* . . . all human love was to me a symbol of divine love; . . . human love was in my eyes a piteous failure unless as an image of the supreme Love which gave meaning and reality to its seeming insanity."[46] The respite at Pantasaph, affording female affection, country rambles, philosophical and theological discourse with the monastics, and, especially, significant reduction in his use of laudanum, revitalized Thompson's poetic talent remarkably. He wrote a substantial number of new poems and prepared the manuscripts and proofs for his first volume, *Poems,* published in December 1893.

His last amorous relationship kindled on a visit from Pantasaph to London in the summer of 1896. It was to exert a more devastating effect on his life and poetry. He fell in love with a vivacious author of sentimental short stories, Katherine Douglas King, whom he met at the Meynell house. This love inspired at least twenty-five poems, some quite revealing and moving, only one of which was published in Thompson's lifetime. But the watchful intervention of her mother, and the enlisted aid of Wilfrid Meynell, subverted whatever possibility existed for the ill-starred, drug-addicted poet to undertake the responsibilities of family life.

While his love for Katie was being thwarted, Thompson suffered another personal loss of equal consequence. In November 1896 Coventry Patmore died unexpectedly. He had met Thompson at Pantasaph in 1894 and the two had become intimate friends. They discussed theology, mysticism, literature, poetics—virtually any subject, and Patmore had offered the younger poet an intellectual companionship and inspiration that no one, not even the generous but intellectually more limited Wilfrid Meynell, had ever provided him.[47] Though their association was brief, Patmore's influence on Thompson's poetics, themes, and mystical thought was profound and was fully reflected in his later writings. Patmore's death, following closely upon his offer to nurse Thompson through an indisposition, seriously shocked this man who throughout his life had surprisingly few intimates.[48]

The month following Patmore's death Thompson returned to London apparently determined to win Katie King by demonstrating that he was emotionally and financially responsible. For the next year or so he wrote a remarkable number of essays, reviews, and commissioned verse, and also planned to write plays and give lectures.[49] This literary accomplishment failed to achieve his personal goal, however, for Katie married another man.

The disappointment ushered in Thompson's final decade. As a frequent associate observed, the poet began "to look on life as so much dead lift, so much needless postscript to his finished epistle."[50] The losses of Patmore and Katie were exacerbated by disappointments in his poetic career. After winning a fair amount of fame with *Poems*, he saw his second volume, *Sister Songs* (1895), roundly criticized. His third volume (1897), dedicated to Patmore (who never saw it) and prepared when Thompson especially needed success to enhance his suit for Katie, received mixed reviews. Some seemed unduly harsh: his verse was described as "obsolete English suffering from a fierce fit of delirium tremens," "wordy hugger-mugger of ecclesiastical metaphor," and "sanctimonious hyperbole."[51] Neither *Sister Songs* nor *New Poems* sold especially well, and a fourth volume in preparation was apparently rejected by his publisher.[52]

By 1900 Thompson recorded that he was using up to five ounces of laudanum each day. From this point his life was a series of missed appointments, tardy manuscript submissions, accidents, and minor tragedies. At the same time he nonetheless continued to produce a large body of prose—more than 250 articles and reviews between 1901 and 1904—on subjects as diverse as literature, cricket, warfare, and politics. These essays are impressive in quality as well as quantity. The achievement seems especially notable when one considers his psychological and physical deterioration. Though Thompson from time to time reasserted his desire to publish something significant, his periods of determination were punctuated with despondent declarations that he would soon return to the streets: "I have never lost the intuition that my life must end as it began, in tragedy. . . . out of the depths I came into the world of literature, and back into the depths I must go. God only grant that the final act in the London streets, to which I incessantly look forward, may be brief in its consummating agony."[53]

Thompson's behavior, always extremely introverted, became increasingly erratic in his last ten years. But even in his youth his absorption in private matters made him remote from the company around him. He never hesitated, though, to intrude his concerns on others. Once during a group reading of *Othello* at the Meynell home he interrupted Desdemona's death scene, declaring, "Here's a go,

Mrs. Meynell; I have lost my *Athenaeum* cheque." It was found in another pocket.[54] He came late to dinner when he had been invited to lunch. He missed the wedding of his favorite, Monica Meynell, because he came too early and decided he was too late. Much of his irregular behavior no doubt stemmed from his use of laudanum and from his idiosyncratic work habits, which often kept him awake so late that he slept through the entire day, to the consternation of several landladies. His abstractions produced some near calamities: He burned off the tip of his boot by sitting too near the fire; he began a small fire at the Meynell home by hanging up his coat with a lighted pipe in the pocket—probably the same pipe that started a blaze that entirely gutted his rented room.[55] Such accidents suggest that he was completely removed from the minutiae of life, but many who knew him in his later years lamented that "this singer, who had soared to themes too dazzling for all but the rarest minds" could be so caught up in trivia: "On great subjects he was slow or silent; on trifles he became grotesquely tedious. . . . He would explain nine times what was clear, and talk about snuff or indigestion or the posting of a letter until the room swam round us."[56] Yet those who knew him unanimously affirmed his gentleness, simplicity, dignity, and merit. Nor was he oblivious to his shortcomings—he at least thought about regulating his indolence. He posted his room with reminders that "At the Last Trump thou wilt rise Betimes," and exhorted himself in his notebooks to deliver journalistic commissions more punctually.[57]

In August 1906 Thompson's physical condition seemed so desperate that Meynell arranged for him to board near the Franciscan monastery at Crawley, Sussex. Though he continued to take laudanum, which he received by mail from a London druggist, he there regained a bit of physical and mental vigor and returned to the city once again able to write a weekly review and to work on a commissioned biography of St. Ignatius Loyola, founder of the Jesuits. As early as 1900 Thompson had begun to earn enough with his journalism to pay for his ordinary upkeep, but because of his addiction and his general disposition his editors usually paid him in small installments. For this last major project, the biography of Loyola, he received one pound each time he handed in three pages of manuscript.

A year after the removal to Crawley Meynell organized a final sojourn away from London and—he vainly hoped—laudanum. He sent the exceedingly feeble poet to the Sussex estate of his friend Wilfrid Scawen Blunt. The countryside and solicitude at Newbuildings could not combat Thompson's advanced state of tuberculosis and drug addiction, however, and his host soon notified Meynell that Thompson might die at any moment. Even here, when Blunt thought his mind was virtually defunct, Thompson completed his last review, a lucid and sound study of the recently republished works of Sir Thomas Browne. In October the poet returned to London; the next month he entered a hospital. The admitting records cited his condition as "morphomania." When he died on 13 November 1907, a month before his forty-eighth birthday, he weighed only seventy pounds. Although opium had no doubt shortened his life, his doctors affirmed that tuberculosis had destroyed one lung and that laudanum may have prolonged his final years. Few mourners attended his funeral. The literary world commemorated his passing with comments as divergent as the critical notices his poetry had received. George Meredith, who had once entertained Thompson for a day, sent roses accompanied by a card: "A true poet, one of the small band." Reports of his death included innuendoes about a lurid life. One Columbia professor is said to have called him, unaccountably, "the poet of sin," and the *Mercure de France* reported that he had gone mad.[58] In the way of personal effects he left very little—a box of newspaper clippings, notebooks, old pipes and pens, and, surprisingly, a cardboard marionette theater like those of his boyhood. He left his manuscript materials and literary estate to Wilfrid Meynell, whose years of monetary and personal assistance were repaid financially by proceeds from posthumous editions of the poet's works.

During his life Thompson never gained the audience he had hoped for: "I am, in [the] present, addressing very few. It would be almost impossible, because quite futile, for me to write were I not convinced that [the] few will one day be [the] many."[59] On another occasion, however, he commented that he wrote not for immediate approval or even for posterity; he wrote because he was by nature a poet: "the public has an odd kind of prejudice that poems are written for its benefit. It might as well suppose that when a woman loves, she bears children for its benefit; or . . . that when a man is hurt, he bleeds for its benefit."[60] Although his poems—and prose—may have been written simply because Thompson's authentic talent demanded expression, modern readers will find among his works true art which deserves a wider audience.

Chapter Two
Poems, "The Hound of Heaven," and Sister Songs

Although Thompson had begun writing verse in his boyhood and continued even during his dereliction in London, he seems not to have found his own voice until he accepted the Meynells' help in regulating his laudanum consumption. According to Wilfrid Meynell, Thompson discovered the legitimacy of his talent when, after his first visit to their home, he read a volume of Alice Meynell's verse and exclaimed, "Then I, too, am a poet!"[1] Though not characteristic of his later verse, his first published poem, "The Passion of Mary," perhaps composed before he left home but revised and submitted to *Merry England* in August 1886 during his stay at McMaster's bootshop, has special poignancy in light of his vagrancy and addiction. It concentrates on the Virgin's pain in "this cold tomb / Of life" before she ascended to the "living throne."

After its April 1888 publication Wilfrid Meynell printed only one other brief poem, "Dream-Tryst," which had arrived in the same soiled manuscript, until after Thompson had endured an agonizing drug withdrawal in a private hospital and then recuperated at the monastery in Storrington. There Thompson began to compose in earnest. From the poetry written at Storrington and later in London he collected his first volume, the 1893 *Poems*.

But the first significant piece of this period, "Ode to the Setting Sun" (published in *Merry England* in September 1889), did not appear in the collection, even though it excited the Meynells so much that they took the train to Storrington to congratulate the poet in person.[2] Their enthusiasm was justified by the poem's linguistic and imaginative intensity and its sonorous and sensuous fusion of classical and Christian motifs to evoke a personal experience of the meaning of Christ's Passion. Stylistically the poem begs comparison with the great odes of Keats, and although it may be deemed imitative and inferior when measured against that standard, it deserves praise for its rich patterning, unity, and vividness.

Thompson encloses the ode proper between a "Prelude" and an "After-Strain," accentuating the music motif sustained through the three parts of the work. The prelude describes a world vibrant with music. Though resounding at evening, the melody does not by design commemorate the sunset, for to the modern world the sun is a deity "discrowned" and consequently no longer hymned in "ancient flatteries." Illuminating a cross that "in this field . . . planted reigns," the "red sun, / A bubble of fire" reveals to the speaker the essential meaning of Christ's Passion. Descriptions of the evening music, the watcher's emotional responses, and the sunset are tightly interrelated by blood imagery that calls up the Passion.

The ode builds upon paradox: the Sun, a pagan god murdered by Christianity, revivifies for the speaker the meaning of the newer religion; the dying sun, touching the cross into a blazing glory, symbolically reveals the rebirth made possible by the Crucifixion. The prelude concludes by invoking the sun to hear the sublime tune of the Passion, "too daring" for Rome and "too dark" for Greece. This song, the ode itself, nicely focuses the paradox in a series of examples from Nature, culminating in a description of the glorious sunset itself, that show death to be the source of life.[3]

Although allusion to the myth of Hyperion, the Titan who attempted to supplant the Olympian sun god, sustains the idea of conflict between the deities of successive ages, Thompson joins the Christian God and the sun as the one creator of all life, from "stealthy-stepping pard" to the "splendid rose." Echoes of "Ode to Autumn" in the description of the rose and numerous instances of synesthesia suggest Thompson's debt to Keats, but his fashioning Christian testimony from vivid sensory details and mythical allusions is distinctly Thompson's own. In the ode proper the speaker's final address to the sun makes explicit its role as "a type memorial" of Christ, again in the blood imagery recurring throughout the poem: "Like Him thou hang'st in dreadful pomp of blood / Upon thy Western Rood."

The poems written at Storrington and after Thompson returned to literary activities in London appeared frequently in *Merry England*, and Wilfrid Meynell by circulating bound reprints of them throughout literary London worked to establish Thompson's reputation. But the first collected volume of poetry materialized only after Thompson was again shipped off to the country to recuperate from narcotic dependency. In retreat at Pantasaph, Wales, Thompson during 1892 finally responded, though not without complaining, to the Meynells' encouragement and to the reminders of his own conscience that a publisher had already advertised his forthcoming collection: "I find Lane has already announced the poems in his booklist; so I am bound to go through with them; else I would let them go to the devil."[4] At Pantasaph Thompson revised works already published and composed new ones for *Poems*, which appeared at the end of 1893. Uneven as it may be, this volume secured him a place in English letters, for it contained "The Hound of Heaven."

Oddly, neither the poet nor his advisor Meynell seems fully to have recognized the superiority of "The Hound of Heaven" to other poems in the volume, for they placed it modestly among a group of "Miscellaneous Poems." Featured more prominently is a sequence of seven lyrics with an epilogue addressed to Alice Meynell, collectively entitled *Love in Dian's Lap*. The sequence is preceded by a dedicatory poem praising both Wilfrid and Alice Meynell as the source of his verse. Thompson frames his indebtedness in a delicate series of analogies patterned as a syllogism: "If the rose in meek duty / May dedicate humbly / To her grower the beauty / Wherewith she is comely," then "To you, O dear givers! / I give your own giving." The simplicity and sincerity of both the sentiment and its expression contrast the dedication with the elaborate and often stilted series that follows.

Love in Dian's Lap

Love in Dian's Lap has rarely been adequately appreciated. It has been termed "a long string of ingenuous, but frigid compliments, barren conceits and emotional absurdities," "hyperboles, chill conceits and stale bombast."[5] Yet Thompson himself thought well of the sequence. Begun in the summer of 1890 soon after he began his detoxification, the sequence fares better critically if it is judged not according to nineteenth- and twentieth-century aesthetics, but according to the conventions of courtly love literature as found particularly in Renaissance lyrics and sonnet sequences, on which it is obviously modeled. Artificial in the sense of being consciously artful, the poems feature archaic language that derives not only from Renaissance poetry but from scripture and liturgy, as well as startling metaphors, sometimes formulated as sustained conceits and sometimes erupting in a vivacious barrage. The verbal wit and invention, elaborate diction and imagery, even the uncurbed word coinages and unabashedly mixed metaphors of the verse are robust expressions of the Renaissance or Baroque aesthetic rather than eccentric ineptitude. The sequence may also reflect the influence of Dante Gabriel Rossetti and the Pre-Raphaelites in the diction and the fusion of sensual and religious imagery. The poems of *Love in Dian's Lap* may in fact be viewed as interesting and often successful stylistic and metaphoric experiments by a novice poet.

Thompson establishes his worshipful posture and the remoteness of his subject, the adored lady, in the first poem, "Before Her Portrait in Youth." The spiritual nature of their relationship is suggested by her physical inaccessibility, emphasized not only by the language (he is "banished" from the lady's face), but also by the fact that here and in the last lyric of the sequence he contemplates not the lady but her portrait. Implying the chasteness of both "courtly" love and Marian worship, this motif also suggests that the real subject is art as much as it is a human relationship. Regarding a painted image of the lady, the speaker imagines her past history. He is consciously depicting imaginative devisings rather than actual experience.

Although the speaker fits the traditional pattern of the courtly lover, worshipping "in very lowlihead of love," he introduces an innovation to the convention by characterizing the youthful portrait that he adores as an "outworn vesture" of the lady that "cheats" the lover, much as the aroma of dying flowers abuses the senses. Aware that he is being deluded by an image of something that is actually dead and gone, the poet can merely "dream the flower" from "dead youth's scent." Thus the lyric ultimately says less about the lady herself than it reveals about the poet's imaginative creating. He is making "colorful dye," something tangible, out of a divine abstraction.

Identifying the lady as a poet, the second poem continues the conventions of courtly love and also the underlying theme of artistic crafting. In "To a Poet Breaking Silence" (published in the August 1893 *Merry England*) the speaker, as in the preceding poem, imagines a history for the lady, this time a raptly religious girlhood. He compares her youthful heart to a blossom "That in darkness did unbosom, / Those fire-flies of God to invite." Her religious concentration need not limit her poetry, he argues, for having forsaken the mountain of the Muses for Sinai, she can continue to write poetry enriched by both religious piety and classical amplitude: "Teach how the crucifix may be / Carven from the laurel-tree, / Fruit of the Hesperides / Burnish take on Eden-trees." These sentiments characterize Thompson's own poetry, which freely blends Catholic mysticism and doctrine with pagan sensuousness and myth.

Having first considered a painting and fictive versions of the lady's life story and then having viewed her as a poet, the sequence in *"Manus Animam Pinxit"* celebrates her as one who has "fashioned" the speaker's soul. Thompson follows his own prescription in the previous poem, for he praises the lady's Christian spirituality by alluding to classical myth. He pointedly remarks the correspondence, which supplies the title of the sequence, between his lady and the chaste Diana, stressing the purity of his devotion to her: "This soul which on your soul is laid, / As maid's breast against breast of maid." She has so much influenced him that he can now mirror Diana's own pure image back to her.

The speaker illustrates the lady's beneficent influence on him in a series of metaphors: She arms him against the campaigns of Hell, protecting a "breach of Heaven's assaulted wall"; she is the soil in a narrow cleft from which he, a sapling, grows; she is the summer that wooes him, the swallow, from the frozen north and prompts his "sunning song." At moments these graceful comparisons contrast with images of starker realism, creating an effect similar to that of John Donne's forceful commonplaces. If the lady, as summer, should withdraw "sanctuary," he the swallow

> from your mind's chilled sky
> . . . needs must drop, and lie with stiffened wings
>
> Among your soul's forlornest things;
> A speck upon your memory, alack!
> A dead fly in a dusty window-crack.

The fourth lyric develops the bird imagery of the third. Called "A Carrier-Song" (published in the September 1893 *Merry England*), it represents the speaker's songs as carrier pigeons that home to the lady. Since she has "waned from us," he is "a darkened cage / Song cannot hymn in." He has only this one poor verse to send her as "carrier" of his message, a "poor tarrier" lingering in his "spirit's eaves" where many wings used "to rustle." Thompson heightens the flight imagery by depicting the spirits of the lady and himself as angels. Wherever hers goes, his angel follows. Consequently he is now "left guardianless," for "Heaven, when you went from us, / Went with my songs too." Beneath the plaintive message of this supplication runs a lighter undercurrent established by brief lines, feminine rhymes and rhythms, and playful imagery. The lady parallels Heaven's Queen in that they both assume the sorrows of others, each becoming a "Mater dolorum." Called an "envious coveter / Of other's grieving," the lady returns to the speaker with contrite smiles, now a "penitent" admonished to "Render your stolen self, / And be forgiven!" The ludic spirit also animates the refrain of each stanza which suggests that seraphim, who desire to celebrate the lady, can learn from the speaker how to praise her properly. One of the most graceful lyrics of *Love in Dian's Lap*, "A Carrier-Song" shows greater control over metaphor and diction than many of Thompson's poems.

Continuing the motif introduced in "A Carrier-Song" that the speaker's "angels" depart with the lady, *"Scala Jacobi Portaque Eburnea"* works variations on this image. Like the ladder of Jacob's dream in Genesis, the lady's soul provides direct access to Heaven. When she is "drawn up from me," the poet laments, all his angels, ascending with her, look down at him from heaven, "Like pent children, very wistful, / That below a playmate see." Although the lady's "dream-dispensing face" has endowed him with wings, his angels' desertion deprives him of these "filmy traffickers" whose "amethyst / Trepidations have foregone me."

"Gilded Gold" returns to a concern with the lady's physical appearance announced in the introductory portrait poem, elaborating clothing imagery employed in the first three poems of the sequence. It develops the conceit that the lady's wearing decorative dress and ornamentation is merely gilding what is already gold. An elaborate praise of her natural graces and essential nature expressed in rich linguistic play, the poem recalls comparably ingenious Renaissance lyrics in which clothing either enhances or belies moral character. As in other poems of the sequence the speaker associates the lady with the Virgin, whose natural beauty was "slurred" by the futile trappings or "braveries" added by worshippers who vainly sought to enhance her inherent splendor.

The concern in "Gilded Gold" with the lady's spiritual beauty, which is reflected but never matched in her physical pulchritude, provides the theme of the seventh poem of the series, "Her Portrait." With the introductory portrait poem it "frames" the sequence. Much longer than the others, this uneven lyric often displays inept, exaggerated imagery and diction and strained sentiment. Yet the poem has a nicely unified conception. Its first lines introduce metaphors of language to establish the poet's inability to describe her adequately. One would need "heavenly grammar," speech turned to gold by angels' tongues, or the pre-Babel language of the Earthly Paradise to do her justice. Finally, her nature is simply ineffable: "Now all is said, and all being said,—aye me! / There yet remains unsaid the very She."

One of the poem's most interesting features, in light of this focus on the inadequacy of speech, is the tension between the spiritual attraction the poet articulates and the physical attraction he obviously feels but specifically denies. More than the other poems of the sequence, "Her Portrait" expresses the frustration so often apparent in courtly love poetry as spiritual language camouflages or renders impotent the speaker's potent physical interest in the lady. Enumerating her physical attributes that he cannot describe in the common language appropriate to other women—cheek, lip, limb, bosom, hair, eyes—the speaker makes us aware of the sensuousness submerged in his strenuously vocalized metaphysical devotion.

Using metaphors that link this poem to the preceding "Gilded Gold," he avers that he has responded physically to other women: "The rustle of a robe hath been to me / The very rattle of love's musketry." But although this lady has of necessity assumed the "flesh, the sexual veil, / Of her sad . . . sisterhood," she wears the sexual guise "which founding Eve indued" as though it were the chaste garb of a nun, a "habit of cloistral flesh." Because "she wears that body" as one dons "a robe, half careless, for it is the use," he "knows" her only as a "votaress to the virgin Sanctitude." This play on the biblical sense of a man's knowing a woman implicitly accentuates the unstated tension underlying what he has insisted in inadequate speech.

Interesting as the poet's complex feelings for the lady may be, frequent lapses in diction mar "Her Portrait." For example, the description of womankind as the "aboriginal sisterhood" of Eve, or the statement that Heaven gives the lady the "use" of trust and us the "usufruct" illustrate Thompson's straining for lofty effect at the expense of clarity or depth of thought and feeling.

An "Epilogue" concluded *Love in Dian's Lap* in its first published form. The subtitle, "To the Poet's Sitter, Wherein he excuseth himself for the manner of the Portrait," continues the motif of portraiture

announced in the first poem and reiterated in the last. The epilogue
contrasts significantly with "Her Portrait" by suggesting the personality of a real woman, for it anticipates the lady's tolerant but modestly self-disparaging reaction to the extravagant praise of the
preceding sequence.

Love in Dian's Lap may be judged a technical tour de force;
throughout the sequence Thompson shows considerable virtuosity
with meter and stanzaic patterns. The heroic couplets of the epilogue,
for example, purposely invite comparison with the poetry of Alexander Pope. The epilogue reaffirms the superiority of the lady in what
appears to be a more rational, analytical manner than elsewhere marks
the highly emotive sequence.[6]

Although these seven poems and epilogue constituted the entire sequence Love in Dian's Lap as it first appeared in the 1893 Poems, Wilfrid Meynell's collected edition prepared after the poet's death added
four other poems, making "Epilogue to the Poet's Sitter" a postscript
to "Her Portrait." Meynell restored a simple four-line epigraph entitled "Domus Tua," which Thompson, at the Meynells' suggestion,
had canceled in the printer's proof of Poems.[7] "Domus Tua" recapitu-
lates in greater clarity the tension between the poet's physical and
spiritual attractions to the lady. It acknowledges that the body of the
perfect woman is the Temple of God, then announces that the poet
would fully avow to God, "I have loved the beauty of Thy house," a
phrase clearly susceptible of double meaning.

"In Her Paths," written in 1890 and published in the July 1893
Merry England, may also originally have been intended for Love in
Dian's Lap. Discrepancies between its form in print and in manuscript suggest that the Meynells did not much like the work as
Thompson first produced it. The lyric reiterates some of the image
patterns of the sequence, using clothing references to demonstrate the
lady's nonphysical beauty. The poem pays tribute to the woman in a
double role as lofty inspiration and nurturing mother.

"After Her Going" again remarks the lady's inspiriting effect on
the world; she can transform even the poet's sadness at her departure.
Thompson wrote both "After Her Going" and the next poem, "Beneath a Photograph," later than Love in Dian's Lap and printed them
in Ultima, a sequel to the earlier sequence printed in his 1897 collection. But the two poems clearly echo the themes and patterns of Love
in Dian's Lap. "Beneath a Photograph," written in playful tetrameter
couplets, wryly contrasts with the more florid portrait poems that

framed the original sequence. Here the speaker contemplates an image of the lady captured by modern photographic equipment rather than by the creative endeavors of a portrait artist. The poem suggests the comparative superiority of traditional, mythical art by characterizing the photographic process, depending as it does on light, as the painting of Phoebus Apollo, whose "white fingers" "Set my Fair's sigh-suggesting" image in the photograph. The antithesis between romantic apprehensions of the lady and this modern, mechanically produced representation is suggested by the seeming reluctance of the "Vesper-like face, its shadows bright / With meanings of sequestered light" to exhibit itself in the photo. The final lines laughingly assert that "all-viewing" though the sun may be, the poet, who learned "art divine" from Apollo, "saw further here than he; / And, Master gay, I swear I drew / Something the better of the two!" These final words of the entire sequence invite us to view the lyrics as Thompson's entries in a poetic painting competition.

The mixed tones and the self-conscious concern with technique in *Love in Dian's Lap* keep it from being powerful poetry. But the sequence clearly establishes Thompson's virtuosity, his devotion to antecedent styles and poets, and his energetic, expansive experimentation—attributes which he cultivates in *New Poems.*

Miscellaneous Poems

The central group of "Miscellaneous Poems" in the 1893 volume includes six works unrelated to each other in content or form. "Dream-Tryst" is the earliest, probably composed like "The Passion of Mary" during Thompson's brief respite from vagrancy at McMaster's bootshop and published in *Merry England* in May 1888. Apparently modeled on Dante Gabriel Rossetti's "Insomnia" and bearing traces of the influence of "The Blessed Damozel,"[8] the relatively uninteresting short lyric sketches a situation recurring frequently in Thompson's verse: a lover longs to unite with a remote, idealized, even perhaps mystical lady. Here the speaker's soul achieves a brief reunion, but only in a dream, with the soul of his dead lady Lucidé, a figure perhaps inspired by Thompson's youthful infatuation with Lucy Keogh, a schoolfriend of his sister.[9]

"A Fallen Yew" draws on his past more artfully. Published in the January 1892 *Merry England,* the series of triplets eulogizes a magnificent old yew that had been felled ("Hacked like dull wood of every day") on the playing field of Ushaw. "Corrival of the world's great prime, / Made to un-edge the scythe of Time," the yew has mythological associations with dryads, Scandinavian "Asgard lords," and the rivers of the classical underworld. Yet the tree was also a merely mutable feature of the commonplace world. It provided a hiding place for boys, a nesting place for birds.

Thompson unifies the mythic and temporal views of the tree by associating both with man. The essential nature of the tree always remained unknown: "But bird nor child might touch by any art / Each other's or the tree's hid heart, / A whole God's breadth apart." Similarly, man's secret self cannot be probed—even by a beloved wife; he has an inner being accessible only to God. While the imagery thus possesses a thematic integrity, discordant tones and affected language mar the poem.

More interesting is "A Judgment in Heaven," written in the summer of 1892 and published in *Merry England* in October 1893. It describes a renowned poet and a ragged rhymer arriving together in Heaven. Thompson's footnote in the 1893 edition identifies the poem as a metrical experiment. In each long line an asterisk marks a caesura, "after the manner of the old Saxon section-point." Although he claimed to be emulating early metrics, Thompson distinguished the tone of his poem from the general somberness of Old English verse by using, instead of Old English alliteration, a system of internal rhymes falling before the caesura, and by frequently having the first half-lines rhyme with each other in feminine rhythm, contrasting with the usually masculine end rhymes binding the stanzas of triplets:

> Athwart the sod which is treading for God * the poet paced
>   with his splendid eyes;
> Paradise-verdure he stately passes * to win to the father of
>   Paradise,
> Through the conscious and palpitant grasses * of intertangled
>   relucent dyes.

The internal rhyme and rhyming first half-lines set up a light undercurrent playing against the steady movement of the long lines.[10] This witty metrical tension corresponds to the thematic contrast established in the poem between the revered poet and the insubstantial rhymer.

The lofty poet, "roseal-chapleted, splendent-vestured," is standing before the divine throne when the celestial throng spies "a wonder! see, * clasping the singer's glories clings / A dingy creature, even to laughter * cloaked and clad in patchwork things." Despite the rhymer's shabby appearance, the poet honors him for approaching Heaven so honestly, for the poet's own splendid vestments and literary skill, actually God's gifts, camouflage the meager self that he like the lesser writer brings to judgment. He pays homage to the rhymer as the more honest man, who "Better . . . wov'st thy woof of life * than thou didst weave thy woof of song." At this point the compassionate Mary Magdalen recognizes the hidden suffering of the superficially splendid poet, who has worn a tormenting hair shirt and crown of thorns beneath his beautiful robes and laurel crown, and God receives both men as "two spirits greater than they know."

An epilogue in straightforward tetrameter couplets and simple language underscores the message implicit in the more elaborate poem proper. Men, misled by appearances, cannot fathom God's wisdom, and they judge both themselves and their fellows improperly: "God . . . grant, at His assize, / He see us not with our own eyes!" Furthermore, "There is no expeditious road / To pack and label men for God, / And save them by the barrel-load." The disreputable rhymer endured only ordinary cares, whereas the apparently favored poet "with a double burthen grieved; / The life of flesh and life of song." Each, however, experienced "deep austerities of strife" simply because each "lived *his* life!"

Critics have related this poem to Thompson's view of himself as one who perhaps failed as a man but attained significance as a poet, and also to his views expressed in the essay "Shelley," composed at the same time Thompson was writing "A Judgment in Heaven" though not published until 1908. The essay suggests that Thompson saw Shelley as "one whose idealistic sufferings as an artist might well be thought of as expiations for the sins of his life."[11] These biographical correspondences are doubtless valid, but the title and situation of the poem also suggest literary comparison with "The Vision of Judgment" by Byron, whom Thompson mentioned in that essay on Shelley and considered "a great satirist."

In "The Vision of Judgment" Byron had satirized Robert Southey's "A Vision of Judgment," which depicted King George III's entering Heaven. Byron's satire shifts the focus to Southey, the Poet Laureate, speaking before the heavenly throne and blatantly revealing his egotistical hypocrisy.[12] Thompson's poem hardly satirizes Byron's satire, but it may purposefully reapply the situation in Byron's poem. Byron's Southey, a crowned and splendid figure, is actually a mere rhymer as well as an arrogant hypocrite. Thompson charitably revises Byron's scathing criticism by dividing this figure into two components, the hypocritical public image and the inferior but unpretentious rhymster, each of whom is treated generously. Whereas Byron's Poet Laureate usurps the role of divine judge by declaring to all: "You shall / Judge with my judgment! and by my decision / Be guided who shall enter heaven or fall," Thompson's laureate has in secret judged himself harshly, only to discover that God evaluates more charitably. Thus Thompson's poem may be seen as cleverly revising Byron's satiric view of mortal and divine judgment on men and poets. "A Judgment in Heaven" asserts that human charity should emulate God's.

Similar sympathy for human weaknesses condemned by men but forgiven by God underlies the first of the miscellaneous poems, "To the Dead Cardinal of Westminster." Published in *Merry England* in February 1892 and written in January within a few days of the death of Cardinal Henry Manning, whom Thompson had once met, the poem is a singular elegy in that it says so little about its ostensible subject. Devised as an address to the cardinal in Heaven, the poem focuses on the speaker's own seeming inadequacies and his hope that devotion to poetry may ultimately compensate for his failings as a man.

On the basis of Thompson's impassioned review (1891) of General William Booth's *In Darkest England,* Cardinal Manning had thought the poet would help implement his own vision of improving the plight of London's workers. When Thompson answered the cardinal's summons to a meeting, however, Manning's surprise at the poet's lack of force and direction must have been evident and disturbing. The verse commemorating the cardinal's death registers Thompson's sense of unworthiness in the churchman's sight. Strikingly, though, this apparent apology for his unworldliness obliquely celebrates the poet's devotion to his art: "he lives detachèd days; / He serveth not for praise; / For gold / He is not sold."

A dramatic monologue, the poem rather strikingly calls to mind the work of Browning in that it implicitly urges readers to reassess their initial inclination to condemn the speaker.[13] The poet imagines how his auditor within the poem will judge him, and in articulating that imagined criticism he implicitly discredits it. By the time he beseeches the spirit of the cardinal to "teach my unripe age. / Tell! / Lest my feet walk hell," readers have probably concluded that he may be treading a sure path to Heaven. Whereas "To the Dead Cardinal of Westminster" seems stronger by association with Browning's monologues, "A Corymbus for Autumn" is impressive for its dynamic individuality. Published in *Merry England* in March 1891, the poem declares itself in its title to be a garland (*corymbus* in Latin designates clusters of fruit or flowers) celebrating the bounty of the harvest season. Critics have judged that "the theme was lost amid what Thompson's friends . . . called the 'foam and roar' of his phraseology.' "[14] Actually, however, the "foam and roar" is precisely the theme, for the poem captures the fecund energy and superfluity of autumn in a dizzying rush of words. Thompson's heady verbal effects convey the speaker's intoxication with the delights of the season, a parallel suggested also by the imagery of drunkenness associated with the grape harvest.

The entire world is "foolish, hazed, / Rubicund, dazed, / Totty with thine October tankard." Thus intoxicated, earth waxes passionate for autumn, personified as a ruddy, wild maiden whose veins pulse with "Umbered juices, / And pulpèd oozes / Pappy out of the cherry-bruises." Far from being "obvious absurdities," the hyperbolic sound effects and extravagantly sustained conceit of the world's drunken indulgence in autumn's bounties almost perfectly match sound to the sense of the poem. From the beginning lines the work conveys the exhilarating effect of plenty in exuberantly abundant alliteration and rhyme, often arranged in couplets and triplets; in the rich variety of quickly clipped phrases energetically punctuating fast-paced longer lines; in lilting, often feminine, rhythms; and in mythological allusion: "Hearken my chant, 'tis / As a Bacchante's, / A grape-spurt, a vine-splash, a tossed tress, flown vaunt 'tis!" The effects often delight both the reader's mind and vocal chords, as when the rosy glow of autumn infectiously colors even the pale moon, "Until it crust / Rubiginous / With the glorious gules of a glowing rust." Hardly poetry out of control, "A Corymbus for Autumn" cavorts splendidly and purposefully.

"The Hound of Heaven"

Though not featured in the volume, the true showpiece of *Poems*— and for many readers, of Thompson's entire corpus—is "The Hound of Heaven," which combines the intensity and daring imagery of his best works with an originality, control, and concentration often lacking in his lesser verse. Begun in December 1889 at Storrington, where he endured excruciating psychological trial with his narcotic withdrawal, it was probably finished in late February 1890 and was published in *Merry England* in July. The ode relates the terror of an unworthy man who flees in panic from the God he desperately needs.

Thompson's most striking achievement in the poem was to identify God as the relentlessly pursuing Hound of Heaven, a designation he wisely confined to the title but reiterated in the poem itself by describing the unshakable tracker of men through two synecdoches—an admonishing voice and pursuing feet. Repetition heightens the fugitive's fear of this pursuer. The opening lines describe his life span and emotions as a landscape through which he rushes:

> I fled Him, down the nights and down the days;
> I fled Him, down the arches of the years;
> I fled Him, down the labyrinthine ways
> Of my own mind; and in the mist of tears
> I hid from Him, and under running laughter.
> Up vistaed hopes I sped;
> And shot, precipitated
> Adown Titanic glooms of chasmed fears,
> From those strong Feet that followed,
> followed after.

A varying refrain intensifies the speaker's panic. He cringes beneath the "instant" feet and the beating voice that intones, "All things betray thee, who betrayest Me," "Naught shelters thee, who wilt not shelter Me," "naught contents thee, who content'st not Me," and "all things fly thee, for thou fliest Me!" With other repetition (for example, God single-mindedly tracks him "with unhurrying chase, / And unperturbèd pace, / Deliberate speed, majestic instancy"), the refrain deftly builds the speaker's sense of the inexorable.

Fleeing blindly, the wretch recognizes few of God's attributes. But besides using pronouns that refer to the Hound of the title, the speaker identifies the inescapable hunter as a "Designer infinite" and "tremendous Lover." This recognition of God's beneficence and creativity lingers in the speaker's consciousness even as he flees. Paradoxically, divine love drives the unworthy man away, for he fears that such love must consume one so paltry as himself by denying him other joy: "(For, though I knew His love Who followèd, / Yet was I sore adread / Lest, having Him, I must have naught beside)."

Feeling himself the prey of an ineluctable and voracious creature-creator, the wretch seeks more limited but accessible affiliations with men and women. But they spurn him, for as God tartly observes, "'none but I makes much of naught' (He said), / 'And Human love needs human meriting.'" The voice brutally underscores the fugitive's lack of merit: he is "Of all man's clotted clay the dingiest clot." For affection the pitiful man turns to nonjudgmental children and to Nature. Desiring childish innocence himself, he petitions Nature, a "poor stepdame," to suckle him on the milk of tenderness, but she cannot "slake" his "drouth." Eventually his childish dependency procures from God the nurturing he needs. Diminishment necessarily precedes growth. As God teaches His child:

> All which I took from thee I did but take,
> Not for thy harms,
> But just that thou might'st seek it in My arms.
> All which thy child's mistake
> Fancies as lost, I have stored for thee at home.

But this restoration occurs only after torment described as a sensuous, even implicitly erotic taming:

> Naked I wait Thy love's uplifted stroke!
> My harness piece by piece Thou hast hewn from me,
> And smitten me to my knee;
> I am defenceless utterly.
> I slept, methinks, and woke,
> And, slowly gazing, find me stripped in sleep.

Thompson suggests the purpose of this erotic humiliation by alluding to the story of Samson, whose sexual enslavement preceded his vanquishing the enemy by toppling the temple:

> In the rash lustihead of my young powers,
> I shook the pillaring hours
> And pulled my life upon me; grimed with smears,
> I stand amid the dust o' the mounded years—
> My mangled youth lies dead beneath the heap.

God mockingly affirms that destruction must precede redemption; before the "strange, piteous, futile thing" will turn to Him, his world must be "marred, / Shattered in shard on shard." Thompson used related imagery in a passage that appears in the printer's proofs, but was canceled just before publication, a passage suggesting the fugitive's attraction to a goodness from which he feels himself excluded. He adopts the posture of a destructive child peering in the window of Heaven:

> I grazed
> Too closely Thy blue window as I gazed,
> Jutted a careless elbow through clear Heaven
> And gashed me with the splinters,—see, I bleed.

Finally the speaker wonders at his own responsibility for the terrors of the flight, formulating this uncertain awareness as a question: "Is my gloom, after all, / Shade of His hand, outstretched caressingly?" The final lines suggest his salvation by modifying the terrifying refrain: " 'Ah, fondest, blindest, weakest, / I am He Whom thou seekest! / Thou dravest love from thee, who dravest Me.' " Thompson in the fair copy of the poem had left the speaker's plight unresolved by using the present tense in this final line, but in the published version, although the speaker remains tentative, God certifies that his flight has ended. Despite this positive conclusion, the poem is most powerful when it evokes the wretch's abysmal guilt and his terror of transcendent mysteries.

Critics have pointed out many sources for "The Hound of Heaven," ranging from general philosophical influences to specific metaphoric and verbal debts. Thompson echoes the religious writings of St. Augustine, St. John of the Cross, St. Ignatius, Silvio Pellico, and scripture. English literary sources include Herbert, Milton, Blake, Wordsworth, Coleridge, De Quincey, Byron, Keats, Tennyson, Rossetti, Swinburne, and even a biography of Browning that Thompson was reviewing while he wrote the poem. Shelley may be his most conspicuous source. "Epipsychidion," which describes the poet's cosmic flight to discover his ideal being, contributed specific language as well as the metaphor of the poet's standing "at bay, / Wounded and weak and panting." And *Prometheus Unbound,* which records the hero's release from torment through discovering love, refers to hounds pursuing their prey through the cosmos.[15] These sources of inspiration notwithstanding, "The Hound of Heaven" remains startlingly original and powerful, deserving Thompson's own judgment that it was "certainly, with all its faults, the greatest of my odes."[16]

Poems on Children

Thompson's acquaintances frequently remarked his childlikeness, a naïveté and remoteness from the disciplined adult world, that was manifested as both thoughtless self-absorption and a disarming innocence and ingenuousness. These traits and anecdotes about his dealings with children help to explain his concentration on childhood in so many poems. "Poems on Children," the last section of the 1893 volume, includes five such works, four of them about the Meynell children and all but one recalling specific events and conversations. In each, childish innocence provides a contrast to adult consciousness of pain, failure, mutability, and mortality.

Although "Daisy," written in 1889 and printed in *Merry England* in March 1890, records an actual conversation that apparently touched the poet rather deeply and avoids the extremes of diction and imagery so pronounced in Thompson's verse, it lacks emotional intensity. The poem suggests the natural setting and the festive mood of a walk the poet took with a little girl he met at Storrington: "Two children did we stray and talk / Wise, idle, childish things." After his companion gives him three gifts—a ripe raspberry, a "guileless look," and a "still word"—he sorrowfully recognizes that such precious moments are fleeting:

> She went her unremembering way,
> She went and left in me
> The pang of all the partings gone,
> And partings yet to be.

A simple poem written in ballad stanzas and obviously modeled on Wordsworth, its poignancy is vitiated by a trite conclusion: "we are born in other's pain, / And perish in our own."

More original and successful is a poem written about a year later and derived from a similar situation, a walk with a young companion whose spontaneous gift prompted the poet to contrast a child's whimsy with the adult's somber reflectiveness. Unlike "Daisy," "The Poppy" achieves distinction through fresh imagery which acquires a richly symbolic dimension.

Dedicated "To Monica," Thompson's favorite of the Meynell children, the poem memorializes an outing when on a "swift child's whim" she plucked a poppy and, presenting it to him, admonished,

"Keep it, long as you live!" The moment recorded in this poem forcibly contrasts the child's blithe ignorance with the adult's disturbing knowledge. The poem gathers energy from the fertile imagery relating the poppy to natural beauty and youth, to poetry, and to the opium that both inspired and inhibited Thompson's writing. Ironically, in both the moment described in the poem and in his recurring use of opium, "the flower / Of sleep brings wakening to me, / And of oblivion memory." Like a "flushed print" of summer's kiss on the earth, like a "yawn of fire," springing from the grass and fanned by the wind "to flapping flame," the poppy is described in terms suggesting the effects of opium:

> With burnt mouth red like a lion's it drank
> The blood of the sun as he slaughtered sank,
> . . .
> Till it grew lethargied with fierce bliss,
> And hot as a swinked gipsy is,
> And drowsed in sleepy savageries.

For the poet the poppy cannot serve merely as an emblem of enduring love or of pretty flowers and precious moments captured forever. It also symbolizes finitude and mortality. Separated from the child by "twenty withered years," the man laments both the impermanent character of the child's impetuous affection, "frankly fickle, and fickly true," and the vanity of his own efforts as a poet.

But in the final stanzas Thompson invests this recognition of ephemerality and failure with further meaning. He also reinvigorates the hackneyed image of Time as a reaper by depicting himself as a poetic dreamer, inspired by the poppy and like the flower a creature of short-lived beauty. Like the practical wheat which feeds men, both poppy and poet must fall to Time's scythe. But unlike the bread produced by that wheat, which provides physical sustenance, the beauty created by the poet will survive time:

> I hang 'mid men my needless head,
> And my fruit is dreams, as theirs is bread:
> The goodly men and the sun-hazed sleeper
> Time shall reap, but after the reaper
> The world shall glean of me, me the sleeper!

The speaker's self-deprecation as a personal failure takes on ironic coloring in the closing lines where he forecasts his poetic success. The child's flower "In leavèd rhyme lies safe . . . / Sheltered and shut in a nook of rhyme." Thompson literally preserved Monica's gift poppy pressed between the pages of his own copy of *Poems.* But the flower is more meaningfully "shut" in the lines of this poem itself. As the preserver of such beautiful objects and moments, the failed man succeeds as poet:

> *I* fall into the claws of Time:
> But lasts within a leavèd rhyme
> All that the world of me esteems—
> My withered dreams, my withered dreams.

Another poem addressed to Monica Meynell, influenced by Coventry Patmore, articulates the frustration of an adult powerless to avert a beloved child's death.[17] "To Monica Thought Dying," conceived in February 1892 when the eleven-year-old was seriously ill, records the adult's overwhelming sense of impotent grief. The desolation created by seeing a child's potential squandered without apparent purpose is here communicated as the speaker's ironic recognition that a child, having said or done little that is memorably wise or sweet, will be remembered for trivial comments that mock the grievers' heavy sense of loss. Death in "his terrible dotage" tauntingly repeats the child's casual mention of a cup of chocolate, bought for a farthing and drunk through a straw. The mourner's observation powerfully redirects his rage against the dying child, who provided Death this mocking litany to recite in the survivors' memory:

> Why have you taught—that he might so complete
> His awful panoply
> From your cast playthings—why,
> This dreadful childish babble to his tongue,
> Dreadful and sweet?

Thus avoiding sentimentality by transforming pain into anger expressed toward the "piteous" but "implacable" dying child, the touchingly understated poem depicts a defense mechanism that allows humanity to cope with grief and powerlessness.

Two other poems addressed to Meynell children avow both Thompson's personal affection for them and his more generalized delight in contemplating childish innocence. Both also contrast that purity with the fallen adult's guilt and sorrow. "The Making of Viola," first published in *Merry England* in May 1892, is contrived as a dramatic dia-

logue spoken by the "Father in Heaven" and echoed by angels as He
calls on the Virgin and Jesus to assist in the sanctified creation of the
infant. God commissions Mary to "spin a tress" and "weave a woof
of flesh to pall" Viola, and asks Jesus to "scoop . . . wood-browned
pools of Paradise" for her eyes and "drown" in them a star. Finally,
the "Lord Paraclete" is directed to "breathe" a "crystal soul" for her.
So created, Viola is borne to earth by angels. The happy air of the
poem (Thompson referred to its "dance-like effects")[18] becomes som-
berly unsettled in the closing references to the infant's entering the
world. During the delivery, "Baby smiled, mother wailed," but the
phrase reverses to commemorate Viola's induction into the pain common to human experience: "Mother smiled, baby wailed." At the end
Viola's "elders" on earth acknowledge that although "Native in your
Heaven is smile," here on earth "you will have weeping-while," for
"Our first gift to you is a / Gift of tears."[19]

Reminiscent of the themes and tones of Blake's *Songs of Innocence
and of Experience,* the work in its dramatic form, simple style, and
characterization of God also recalls medieval English drama.[20] These
kinships to Blake and to medieval literature impart a certain charm
to the poem, but its expression of the general human misery lacks the
force needed to contrast effectively with the gentle fancy of the infant's celestial creation.

The tribute addressed "To My Godchild, Francis M. W. M." (the
Meynells' son born in May 1891 and named to honor the poet) similarly contrasts the unblemished potential of the newborn with the
disillusionment of the adult.[21] The speaker's confusion and anxiety are
suggested by a nautical metaphor opening the poem: Adulthood is
likened to the plight of a "labouring . . . galleon" that has broken
its cable and floated into "the inclement main" of the Arctic but hap-
pily returns to "azure roads again" when the infant, described as a
"white halcyon," alights " 'mid our frozen crew." Disturbed to think
that this precious babe might emulate his namesake, Thompson
hopes the godchild will pattern himself after other men named Francis—Petrarch or the saint of Assisi.

While the poem purports to reveal the speaker's disturbing sense
of unworthiness, its contrived diction, mixed metaphors, and classical
ornamentation prevent its achieving the power of genuinely anguished
self-examination. The work remains a relatively undistinguished occasion piece, memorable only for the final line. Inscribed on Thompson's headstone, it fittingly memorializes not only his poetic

preoccupation with children but also his gentle unworldliness: "Look for me in the nurseries of Heaven."

Poems earned many favorable reviews. Although some critics disparaged Thompson's hyperbolic effects, others lavished hyperbolic praise: "by this volume alone he is as secure of remembrance as any poet of the century. . . . it is itself among the great achievements of English poetry; it has reached the peak of Parnassus at a bound." Thompson is "a poet of the first order, . . . a seer and singer of rare genius." Coventry Patmore assessed more judiciously: the volume reveals "profound thought, far-fetched splendour of imagery, and nimble-witted discernment of those analogies which are the roots of the poet's language." The volume sold two thousand copies within six months, and if all readers did not immediately rank Thompson "the first of Victorian poets," most probably concurred with Patmore in judging "The Hound of Heaven" one of the " 'great' odes of which the language can boast."[22]

Sister Songs (1895)

Thompson's next published volume, *Sister Songs*, deservedly drew much harsher criticism. Addressed to two of the Meynells' young daughters, the work is a single long poem in two main parts, with a proem and an epilogue. To suggest its double inspiration and structure, Thompson originally entitled it "Amphicypellon," referring to a cup designed for two users, mentioned by Homer, of a sort he had seen among the Trojan artifacts exhibited by Schliemann at the South Kensington Museum in 1879.[23]

The poem grew out of Thompson's finest feelings of gratitude and devotion to Wilfrid and Alice Meynell. His emotional investment in the poem may have clouded his creative judgment as he wrote, for *Sister Songs* becomes glutted by the characteristics that in moderation distinguished other poetry of the period. Begun during the summer of 1890, during the time he was composing "The Hound of Heaven," it shows none of the discipline by which Thompson in the great ode focused his resourceful figurative invention to a cogent and deeply affecting point. Ostensibly a paean to childhood innocence and Nature, the work also discusses Thompson's concept of ideal womanhood, the pain of a poet's existence, and his own spiritual growth, melancholy, and isolation.

Connections between these subjects become lost in a torrent of verbiage, frequently quite musical, but just as often syrupy and contrived. Sometimes the melody succeeds in spite of its self-consciousness, as in the lilt achieved by an alliterative refrain, "syllabling to Sylvia." From the flood of imaginative metaphors individual images occasionally stand out. Symbolic vividness distinguishes a picture of an Arab traveling through the desert, with "Lean Thirst, lolling its cracked tongue, / Lagging by his side," and "a rusty-wingèd Death" flying before, "Casting ribbèd shadows o'er / The blank desert, blank and tan." More mundane imagery acquires force from concrete detail, especially in the description of grass "warted with rain like a toad's knobbed back."

Several prominent images are poignant in the context of Thompson's life, most notably reference to the generous-hearted prostitute who befriended him: "of her own scant pittance did she give, / That I might eat and live: / Then fled, a swift and trackless fugitive." He utters a touching valediction, comparing himself to a timid child who lovingly presents a frail flower that immediately withers.

Despite his splendid metaphoric resourcefulness, *Sister Songs* displays Thompson's imitativeness (in echoes of Keats, Shelley, and Tennyson which illustrate their superiority to the copy), his giddy absorption in sound effects for their own sake, and his predilection for incongruously inflated language. Although Thompson lacked emotional and artistic control when he wrote the poem and presented it as a Christmas gift in 1890, he eventually developed a sharper sense of its inadequacies. Wilfrid Meynell, however, perhaps wanting to keep Thompson's name before the public, perhaps simply deeply touched by the tribute to his family, finally prevailed on the poet to publish the work.

Soon after it appeared in June 1895 Thompson called it "a bad business which I cannot mend, and wash my hands of."[24] Surprisingly resilient and foresighted, he had written his publisher almost immediately, suggesting the best remedy for this injury to his reputation: "I am not a business man, but my own judgment was against the public printing of the poem until I had a more assured position as a writer. . . . Consequently I had already considered the advisability of following it by a collection of new poems, which I have already commenced to revise for that purpose."[25]

Chapter Three
New Poems

Thompson's continuing embarrassment over *Sister Songs* accentuates his anticipation of starting over, at least in the public view, with his next published collection of verse. Just two weeks after he sent the manuscript for *New Poems* to his new publisher, Constable, in April 1896, he announced its advent to his newly important friend Coventry Patmore: "It should have been my second book" if Wilfrid Meynell "had not frustrated my careful waiting by committing me to the publication of my last ill-starred volume."[1] Besides revising for the forthcoming collection some poems that had already been published in journals, during a six-month period—when he was also editing *Sister Songs* for the press—he wrote about thirty new pieces.[2] A schedule that he prepared to organize his time illustrates his serious desire to regulate not only his writing but also his religious observances and philosophical study.[3] This speculative and logistical discipline contributes a new dimension to the 1897 volume.

Thompson was quite conscious of his new manner. When in May 1896 he asked Wilfrid and Alice Meynell to evaluate the manuscript, he warned them to expect something different: "It is utterly strange to you, will need judging from other standpoints than my work you are used to." But his letter also sounds substantially more confident than his tentative requests for advice about earlier work. He insisted that they not comment on the poetry until they saw it set in proof, for "you have often recast a judgment made on my Ms.; not often, I think, after you had seen my work in print."[4]

But even though Thompson viewed the volume as a departure from his past work, he also saw it as an end:

I believe this will be my last volume of poetry—in any case my last for some years—and I am determined to make it complete, that I may feel all my work worth anything is on record for posterity, if I die. If the book would sell rapidly, like my first, I could divide it; since the publisher would accept another volume. But I know it will not; and I must get it all through now,

for no publisher will be in a hurry to take another from me. It is my poetic
last will and testament; I have been preparing it for three years, and I will
not make it less complete for mere publisher's reasons.[5]

In part his sense that he had exhausted his capacities derived from
uncertainty of how to harmonize the talents that distinguished his
first collection with the virtues he detected in the new: "I have
gained, I think, in art and chastity of style, but have equally lost in
fire and glow. 'Tis time I was silent. This book carries me quite as
far as my dwindling strength will allow; and if I wrote further in poetry, I should write down my own fame."[6]

A Narrow Vessel and Ultima

Two sequences of love poems in the 1897 volume, which was published in May, demonstrate the juxtaposition of new and old elements
in the collection. A Narrow Vessel, the second section of the volume,
speaks realistically of human feelings, while Ultima, the fifth and last
section, continues the manner and matter of Love in Dian's Lap, the
important sequence in the 1893 Poems. Contrasts between A Narrow
Vessel, seven poems plus an epilogue, mostly written in 1894–1895,
and the earlier Love in Dian's Lap highlight the strength of the later
sequence. It has a naturalness of expression and a psychological complexity not found in the stylized experimentation of Love in Dian's
Lap. Such directness causes many readers to view the sequence primarily as the record of an awkward love affair with Maggie Brien, the
daughter in a household where Thompson twice rented rooms during
his stay at the Franciscan monastery at Pantasaph. This romance,
timid and aborted though it may have been, was at least one ingredi-
ent in renewing Thompson's literary productivity after the hiatus following publication of Poems.

Thompson himself was characteristically diffident when alluding to
his relationship with Maggie. In a note written in late December
1892, soon after his arrival in Wales, he quipped about a possible
romance: "I have half a mind, by way of final outrage, to make love
to what I think the loveliest girl I have ever seen. But I have still
some convention hanging about me in a tattered condition. . . ."[7]
Over a year later, in February 1894, he wrote Monica Meynell that
he could not return a photographic proof of himself which her father
had sent, because "a girl at my lodgings" had "gone off with it. I'm

sure I don't know why; for she does not like me, and keeps out of
my way as much as possible. But the ways of girls are unsearchable."⁸
His attempt to explain the inscrutable nature of a young woman's at-
tachments constitutes the series which, despite its autobiographical
basis, Thompson emphatically described as "dramatic."

In keeping with the subtitle of *A Narrow Vessel*, "Being a little dramatic sequence on the aspect of primitive girl-nature towards a love
beyond its capacities," Thompson initially creates the illusion of objectivity by employing dramatic methods in the first two poems. The
first poses as dialogue between the girl in the romance and an older
confidante who considers her a "Cross child." Moreover, the first and
second poems, by giving opposing views of the same situation, present a dialectic rich in dramatic irony. The girl speaking in the first
poem remains naively unaware of the attitudes of the man who in the
second poem evaluates her conduct. But the story of the sequence
does not really unfold through dialogue, nor does the female character
ever speak for herself.

The allusive narrative is focused from the viewpoint of the unhappy
male, as the titles of the first two poems reveal. The young woman's
flirtatious and superficial sense of courtship leads the male speaker to
label her behavior "A Girl's Sin—In Her Eyes" and "A Girl's Sin—
In His Eyes." The "sin" considered by the first pair of poems is the
girl's having given a lock of her hair to the aspiring lover.

In the first poem, ostensibly her words but actually his imagined
account of them, the lover sympathetically interprets the girl's "sin"
merely as thoughtless unsophistication. She is by turns coquettishly
secure of her powers of attraction and nervously uncertain whether she
should have granted the token of her esteem. Confident that even
without speaking he had asked for the lock of hair "with great loud
eyes" that "gazed it from my head," she expects to flaunt her power
over him. Because he has enjoyed this one "privilege," "a thousand
he shall miss!" But she also fears his reactions: "Perhaps he'll think
me light; perhaps— / Perhaps he'll think I—love him!"

Her language, as he imagines, draws on the conventions of Renaissance sonnet sequences in the manner of *Love in Dian's Lap*, depicting
love as mock warfare. Whereas such language and metaphor in *Love
in Dian's Lap* point up both the poet's chaste adoration of an idealized
lady and the conscious artifice of his poetic and linguistic experimentation, the metaphors here reveal the artificial concept of love that the
man attributes to the young woman. In the rest of the sequence the

man uses more natural diction and image to suggest his own, more
sincere brand of loving, which the girl's childish playing at love eventually embitters and destroys.

In the second poem the man opposes the lady's caprice with his
own more serious attitude, yet he continues the military metaphors,
speaking of the "proud surrender" of the lock of hair by a "tender
tyranness." The imagery and pervasive use of paradox remind us that
the ambivalence (and in fact all the sentiments of the first poem) expresses the man's view of the lady. The paradox and imagery and the
quandaries created for the lovers also relate the situation of both versions of "A Girl's Sin" to Alexander Pope's *The Rape of the Lock,* which
likewise satirizes social pretensions and vanity through the conflict
over a sexually euphemistic lock of the lady's hair. Thompson's poem
may be seen to twist the situation of Pope's satire by having the lady
boldly assuage the aspiring lover's desire for a token of her favor,
which he then "worships" as a "brown miracle" and proof of "her shy-
ness free, / Her timorous audacity."

In the third poem of the sequence, "Love Declared," the man's
tone and attitude change markedly. This lyric has been described as
"the only Thompson poem which frankly treats a sexual theme."[9] It
describes a kiss that momentarily transforms their shyly hesitant en-
counters, setting the night aflame and wrapping them in "vibrant
fire." The oblique but obvious sexual imagery (also apparent in the
title of the sequence) directly counters the concept of love as flirtatious poses, which develops in both versions of "A Girl's Sin." The
poem redefines conventional notions of propriety, for her "sin" is neither the sexual encounter of "Love Declared," nor the bold gift of hair
in the first two poems, but the girl's socially circumspect yet insin-
cere play. The poem implies the superiority of genuine physical expressions of love to more socially acceptable strategems of chaste but
coy pursuit and denial.

Thompson relates the moment of passion in dignified blank verse
and images that imply the lovers' transport beyond time. The imagery suggests the rarity of the event: "This moment is a statue unto
Love / Carved from a fair white silence." Yet the beauty and permanence implied by the metaphor are soon qualified by a suggestion that
turbulent passions underlie the lovers' usually controlled facade, trou-
blingly dynamic emotions which cannot be neatly contained in a
static, perfect moment. The feelings released by the declaration of
love resemble "dream's snapped links" which hamper "the limbs / Of

waking." The lovers' apparent calm is as deceptive as a "running evening stream" scarcely perceptible except where "the moon / Is shattered to a creamy flicker of flame."

The fourth poem, "The Way of a Maid," which contrasts the attitudes of the male and female in tongue-in-cheek tetrameter couplets, undercuts the beautiful moment of the preceding poem. The lover, overawed by unexpectedly sinking into "some sudden hollow of sweet," is rendered dumb when he tries to project "utterance great / Up to the miracle of his fate." The woman, however, does not aspire to either lofty expressions or lofty feelings: the "wise girl" is "saved" from "such Icarian fall . . . by her confidence that she's small." Implicitly associating himself with the mythological Icarus, the speaker ostensibly condemns himself for trying to soar above mere mortals in both love and song. The image forecasts his failure in both. But the acid quality of his references to the lady implies the limitations of her narrow vision. "Feeling the infinite must be / Best said by triviality," the girl fritters love's moments of grandeur: "And while she feels the heavens lie bare, / She only talks about her hair." This concluding image trivializes the severed lock of hair which in "A Girl's Sin" both the man and the woman had considered such a significant token of her attachment to him. Similarly, the flight imagery—her expression "bates its wings," shunning the heavens to settle on "little things"—undercuts the man's sense in the preceding "Love Declared" that when they avowed their feelings, "Time's beating wing subsided" and Love alighted "like a bird new-lit . . . / Poised in our quiet being."

The speaker extends the flight metaphor in the next poem of the sequence, "Beginning of End," where he concludes that the woman's reticence reveals her narrowness of feeling: "She was aweary of the hovering / Of Love's incessant and tumultuous wing." "Beginning of End" records a moment when the girl, neglecting an "appointed tryst" with her lover, with "her lightest comrade lightly walked" past him with no acknowledgment.[10] The poem not only emphasizes the girl's idea that courtship involves coy strategems, but also demonstrates her ambivalence—she wants to be loved but not to love, as the wordplay suggests: "She thought not of her lover, deem it not / . . . But she forgot not that he was forgot"; "she must punish him for doing him wrong."

"Penelope" records this ambivalence. The contradictory signs of both her genuine feeling and her heartless coquetry arise from the same source—her faulty idea of loving. Her ambivalence is expressed in an allusion to the story of Penelope, which, like the Icarus story in "The Way of a Maid," works ironically. Whereas in the Odysseus story the faithful wife Penelope discouraged undesired suitors by the strategem of each day weaving a cloth but each night unweaving it, the girl of this sequence has fused the unwanted suitors and the desired husband into the single person of her lover: "For, wild Penelope, the web you wove / You still unweave, unloving all your love."

In seven brief lines "The End of It" judges that the lady foolishly squandered the lovers' relationship. Her "sin" finally differs from the superficial interpretations offered by both versions of "A Girl's Sin," for her real crime is that "She did not love to love; but hated him / For making her to love." The poet attempts to emphasize the objectivity of this analysis of love's failure by dropping the first-person pronoun. Despite this distancing device, "The End of It" passes judgment in language characteristic of the frustrated lover throughout the entire sequence: "Her own self-will made void her own self's will."

A didactic "Epilogue" concluding A Narrow Vessel interprets the physical love relationship in the sequence as an allegory of the trivial human soul's inability to love God properly. In order to refute one reader's criticism of this allegorizing, Thompson explained his symbolic intention:

. . . all love was to me a symbol of divine love; . . . human love was in my eyes a piteous failure unless as an image of the supreme Love which gave meaning and reality to its seeming insanity. The lesson of that sequence is just this. Woman repels the great and pure love of man in proportion to its purity. This is due to an instinct which she lacks the habits and power to analyse, that the love of the pure and lofty lover is so deep, so vast in its withheld emotion, as her entire self would be unable to pay back. . . . So, with instinctive fear, she recoils from a love which her all cannot equal. Though the lover asks no more than she please to give, his love asks her very being, demands a continual upward strain. The narrow vessel dreads to crack under the overflowing love which surges into it. . . . Now this is but the image and explanation of the soul's attitude towards only God.[11]

Although Thompson's explanation of man's unworthy resistance to divine love fits other poems he wrote—"The Hound of Heaven," for example—the abstract "Epilogue" scarcely suits the more concrete sequence to which he affixed it. While the series remains less complex psychologically and aesthetically than Robert Browning's *James Lee's Wife* (1864) or George Meredith's *Modern Love* (1862), it invites comparison with these earlier Victorian sequences by sketching one lover's painful and often bewildered attempt to understand what erodes a love relationship. Thompson's later comment on *Modern Love* indeed summarizes the effect of his own, simpler sequence better than the allegorical explanation he had given for *A Narrow Vessel*: it "delicately" brings out "the peculiar tragedy of modern life—its voicelessness; the way in which the agonies of the soul are suppressed behind a mask of compulsory commonplace, so that the inner self bleeds to death, while the outer self prattles well-bred inanities."[12] *A Narrow Vessel* is distinguished by its candid preoccupation with human love, its psychological and emotional realism, its ironic sensibility, and its tonal and metaphoric unity.

The sequence clearly deserves attention for more than its biographical interest. Yet even on that level it requires two postscripts. Thompson, inexperienced as he was with mature, reciprocal affection, may to some extent have misjudged Maggie Brien's love. She never married, and when she died in October 1907, less than a month before Thompson's own death, the faded proof of his photograph, which she had appropriated in 1894, was discovered behind a picture hanging in her room.

Further, one important fact argues against reading the series as pure autobiography. "Love Declared," the account of a passionate exchange between the lovers, exists in an early version dating from 1889.[13] Although it too may derive from personal experience, probably referring to Thompson's liaison with the London prostitute, its appearance in a sequence written at least five years later and inspired by another woman emphasizes that even in verse that seems to record specific events, Thompson was the self-conscious craftsman on display more flamboyantly in *Love in Dian's Lap*.

Although *A Narrow Vessel* has an artistic integrity often overlooked in biographical interpretations, Thompson himself seems to have undervalued the sequence. He described it as a "sacrifice" to the "levity of the critics." When he sent the manuscript of *New Poems* to Wilfrid Meynell, Thompson judged that in a period reacting against "poetry, mysticism, and everything not Philistine," most of his work was unlikely to appeal to a public that "ever loved what it could read with

one eye shut." *A Narrow Vessel,* he said, was a concession to this taste,
"a whole section of the lightest poems I ever wrote."[14] Although he
may have hoped to camouflage the glimpses of his relationship to
Maggie Brien with these remarks, he seems not to have recognized
the merit of his unpretentious series.

Thompson also seems to have disparaged *Ultima,* the sequence of
love poems which concludes the volume, for in November 1896 he
wrote his publisher Arthur Doubleday that if the book, in proof,
seemed too long, *Ultima* could be omitted. He was not so much deni-
grating the sequence, however, as asserting his authorial control by
insisting that Doubleday retain two translations from Victor Hugo.
These Thompson would keep, "whatever I left out," for "they were
held over from my first book and I will not hold them over again."[15]

The seven poems of *Ultima* (the additional "Envoy" serves as a valediction for the entire volume) may be seen as a sequel to the more
linguistically and metaphorically extravagant *Love in Dian's Lap,* for,
like the earlier series, they express Thompson's devotion to Alice
Meynell.[16] This connection between the two sequences is emphasized
by Wilfrid Meynell's decision, when he was preparing his 1913 collection of Thompson's poetry, to print two poems from the later sequence, "Beneath a Photograph" and "After Her Going," as parts of
Love in Dian's Lap, thus reducing *Ultima* to five poems. Probably begun in the late spring of 1894 following an April visit the Meynells
paid Thompson at Pantasaph, the series sketches a lover's awareness
that his adored lady does not return his regard, and that she will
doubtless abandon him. But unlike the earlier sequence centered on
Alice Meynell, this one implies that the frustrated love relationship
is finally less important than the spiritual awareness his feelings for
the lady have helped the speaker to attain.

The first, and probably most interesting, poem of *Ultima,* "Love's
Almsman Plaineth His Fare," with its single dominant metaphor and
relatively restrained language illustrates the stylistic control of the sequence as a whole. The poem likens the adoring lover, who receives
from the lady only limited gestures of friendship, to a begger grateful
for her charity yet discontent with its meagerness: "A hand-clasp I
must feed on for a night, / A noon, although the untasted feast you
lay, / To mock me, of your beauty." He recognizes his own unworthiness and ingratitude. His "heart all kneaded out of honey and
fire," bound to "an unlovely soul" and "a body nothing worth,"
gnaws itself "for famine's bitterness." Although he continues to praise

the lady, he ends by wishing that she may know the hunger pangs of unrequited love:

> That you might
> Be lover for one space, and make essay
> What 'tis to pass unsuppered to your couch,
> Keep fast from love all day; and so be taught
> The famine which these craving lines avouch!
> Ah! miser of good things that cost thee naught,
> How know'st thou poor men's hunger?—Misery!
> When I go doleless and unfed by thee!

Continuing the courtly and Renaissance flavor of the 1893 *Love in Dian's Lap,* Thompson chose archaic language, finally preferring, for example, the older form "plaineth" to "complaineth of," which he had used in two ink drafts. But the poem derives power from straightforwardness and unity from the controlling metaphor, which deftly implies the lover's ambivalent attitude toward the lady as well as his recognition of the paradox of his situation: an unworthy begger living on unearned generosity, he nevertheless suffers from hunger and consumes himself for want of a more bountiful feast of her favors.

The second poem, "A Holocaust," anticipates the lady's rejecting him to "scourge" his "sloth"[17] in terms that link his devotion to the lady to his devotion to God. He uses the military and religious metaphors familiar in courtly love poetry but applies the language to a nontraditional end. Instead of implying that the lady is his heaven or divinity, Thompson concludes that loving her has brought him closer to knowledge of God. Thus the perplexing title of the poem is effectively redefined, for the holocaust, signifying a holy offering which is totally consumed by fire, initially seems to refer to the speaker himself, consumed as an offering to his lady. Eventually, however, the title applies to his adoration of the lady, which must be sacrificed to a higher love of God.

Although the speaker avows his pain in an egotistical analogy to Christ's solitary anguish on the Mount of Olives, humbler touches, starkly realistic, poignantly anticipate his reaction to her inevitable rejection: "Thou knowest if this heart of flesh / Quivers like broken entrails, when the wheel / Rolleth some dog in middle street." This naturalistic image relates to the epigraph of the poem, "No man ever attained supreme knowledge, unless his heart had been torn up by the roots," but overall the poem lacks both the metaphoric unity and emotional depth of "Love's Almsman Plaineth His Fare."

The next two poems demonstrate the unevenness of purpose in the *Ultima* sequence. Both are considerably lighter in tone than others in the series and break the emotional tension. The sunny contentment of "After Her Going" and the jocular attitude of "Beneath a Photograph"—as well as the kinship of imagery in this last poem to the artistic metaphors of *Love in Dian's Lap*—would seem to justify Wilfrid Meynell's decision to incorporate them in the 1893 sequence.

"My Lady the Tyranness" and "Unto This Last," the following two poems of *Ultima,* emphasize the lady's "tyranny" over the lover, but also suggest that knowing her has fostered his philosophical balance. Of the two, "My Lady the Tyranness" offers the most interesting development of the feudal relationship of courtly love. Depicted in the opening lines as a "half-petulant" and "loving rebel" held in "feodary" subservience to her "sovran sweet rapaciousness," the speaker considers whether he can call anything his own, "Not yours, my love, not yours!" Stanzas that begin defiantly end by asserting the lady's sovereignty over his skies, thoughts, life, death, Heaven, God, and Fame:

> Nay then, I said, I have my thought,
> Which never woman's reaching raught;
> Being strong beyond a woman's might,
> And high beyond a woman's height,
> Shaped to my shape in all contours.—
> I looked, and knew
> No thought but you were garden to.
> All yours, my love, all yours!

The tone of debate established within each stanza communicates the speaker's tension, for the first lines, rejecting the lady's power over all that he has, address himself, whereas the concluding portion of each stanza, acknowledging her pervasive influence, addresses the lady directly.

Eventually the lover, like the speaker in "A Holocaust," discerns the connection between his love of the lady and his knowledge of God. Imagery of food and drink in this poem and the next, "Unto This Last," links both works to the first poem of the sequence. But unlike the imagery in "Love's Almsman Plaineth His Fare," the metaphor in the two later poems reveals not the speaker's dissatisfaction but his recognition that, though she remains unattainable, she succors him. "Ultimum" ends the sequence. It begins with the piquant image of Love dying, lamented by "his offspring songs":

> One lifts his wing, where dulls the vermeil all
> Like clotting blood, and shrinks to find it cold,
> And when she sees its lapse and nerveless fall
> Clasps her fans, while her sobs ooze through the webbèd gold.

The speaker then swears to write no more futile love poetry. Yet as the droll image of sobs oozing through a fan suggests, the tone of this renunciation is less morose than confident. The lover, though disappointed in his suit for personal happiness, has been conducted to love of higher ideals.

Although the *Ultima* sequence exhibits greater formal and tonal consistency, and somewhat less in the way of overwrought imagery and extravagant verbal invention than its predecessor *Love In Dian's Lap*, these apparent virtues actually render the sequel comparatively lifeless. Even the regularity of verse forms—stanzas composed of iambic tetrameter or pentameter couplets or quatrains, for the most part—when compared to the variety and experimentation of *Love in Dian's Lap* make *Ultima* seem rather stodgy. And the sequence seems even weaker when contrasted with the more direct and natural series *A Narrow Vessel*.

Sight and Insight

Despite its limitations, the *Ultima* sequence suggests Thompson's broadened philosophical concerns discernible thoughout much of *New Poems*. Whereas *Love in Dian's Lap* of the 1893 *Poems* primarily used the lover's experience as a vehicle for exploring artistic options, the *Ultima* sequence more consistently employs the amatory situation to adumbrate religious attitudes. This analogy between romantic love and love of God becomes more pronounced in other works written for *New Poems*, especially those in the section that opens the volume, *Sight and Insight*. Recurring use of the metaphor testifies to the strong influence of Coventry Patmore, with whom Thompson developed a close and extremely important friendship between October 1894, when Patmore visited Thompson at Pantasaph (probably at the request of Alice Meynell), and November 1896, when the older poet died—before seeing Thompson's *New Poems* dedicated to himself. Thompson had been familiar with Patmore's work since late 1889, when he first read both the poetry of *The Unknown Eros* and Patmore's first collection of prose, *Principle in Art.* Initially Patmore's poetry, emphasizing human sexuality and written in what has been termed "drily cerebral, unmusical verse," scarcely appealed to Thompson, whose own experience and aesthetic tastes differed substantially.[18] Two factors significantly altered this first reaction, however. Patmore, who was like Thompson passionately devoted to Alice Meynell, in January 1894 published an essentially judicious and appreciative review of Thompson's *Poems.* Although it repeated charges frequently levied against Thompson—intrusive word coinages, lack of control, "intellectual" and therefore unconvincing ardor—the review also praised his "profound thought," "far-fetched splendour of imagery," and "truly splendid command of language." Deeply pleased, Thompson declared that Patmore's review "managed to combine fine praise with discriminate and illuminating criticism of defects and limitations." Unlike other critics, who merely "note the symptoms of one's poetic maladies," Patmore "diagnoses the seat of the disease. I have got more help and self-knowledge from his article than from anything else which has appeared."[19]

But even before reading Patmore's positive review of *Poems,* Thompson was significantly affected by himself preparing a review of Patmore's second collection of essays, *Religio Poetae,* in June of 1893. The review (published in *Merry England* in September) concludes with a judgment that, as John Walsh observes, suggests Thompson's sense of the inadequacy of his own previous work: "One who has had a purely literary training, and has afterwards passed to the treatment of such subjects as occupy *Religio Poetae,* must have experienced a disagreeable surprise. He discovers that the style of literary beauty which had been the pride of his heart, is as useless for his new objects as a butterfly-net for deep-sea fishing."[20] A personal friendship begun by correspondence while Thompson was preparing this review and cemented when Patmore visited Pantasaph sparked Thompson's pursuit of techniques and material better suited to his new sense of purpose. His views on poetic symbolism and meter, especially regarding the importance of accent and pauses,[21] as well as many points of his religious philosophy were confirmed or altered by his contact with Patmore. This influence shows most clearly in the first section of *New Poems, Sight and Insight,* a dozen poems connected by theme and imagery. The major preoccupation of the group is the quest for visions of transcendent truth, as distinguished from merely sensory sight. Thompson shared with Patmore a brand of religious mysticism much akin to Platonism. In *Sight and Insight* he defines the poet as no mere craftsman, but a seeker after truth. "The Mistress of Vision," the first poem of the series—and of the volume—depicts allegorically the speaker's initiation into what it means to be a poet. He learns that he must not only acquire insight rather than sight, but also practice self-sacrifice as exemplified by the Crucifixion.

The speaker learns these lessons from the Mistress of Vision. She derives from a tradition, going back to Plato and transmitted through Boethius, of female figures who allegorically personify such ideals as Reason or Philosophy and instruct the poet in higher truths. Thompson's Lady, who creates and tends an exquisite enchanted garden, may also be influenced by a comparable figure in Shelley's "The Sensitive-Plant."[22] Thompson's fertile garden in the mystical "land of Luthany," "tracts of Elenore," enjoys perpetual spring conjured by the Lady: "the roses were most red, for she dipt them in her heart."

A "mazeful wonder" thrice engirdled by an emerald wall, this garden through many details strikingly evokes the setting of "Kubla Khan"—by Thompson's "favourite poet"[23]—and its symbolic depiction of poetic inspiration. Coleridge's concluding portrait of the speaker who would emulate the damsel with a dulcimer resounds in Thompson's "Lend me, O lend me / The terrors of that sound, / That its music may attend me, / Wrap my chant in thunders round."

Thompson's poem also reveals the influence of "Kubla Khan" in its enigmatic Oriental reference to the Lady's visionary glimpse of a snowy peak on "Himalay" beneath which "peoples underground dwell whom antique fables know . . . Hiding from the shock of Day,"[24] reminiscent of Coleridge's Kubla hearing "Ancestral voices prophesying war." Thompson's imagery in this prophetic passage at first glance seems more enigmatic than Coleridge's, and even faintly ludicrous, until one recognizes the purposeful juxtaposition of contrasts in Thompson's allegory. Many of the lessons the speaker must learn from the Lady are paradoxical: beautiful poetry arises from pain; all apparent discords in the universe conceal essential harmonies; one must achieve insight by relying on intuition more than on optics. These lessons—all essentially Romantic tenets—are embodied in a song uttered by the Lady during a visionary trance, a song the speaker can render only in a few "dim snatches."

The gist of its teaching about the nature of the true poet lies in several stanzas where the Lady associates the poet's wreath with Christ's crown of thorns and Noah's coronal. The song itself, because it is inadequately reconstructed by the speaker of the poem, like Icarus aspires to a significant height that it cannot reach. This combination of mythological and Christian allusion illustrates a concept of symbolism that Thompson had held, though perhaps had not clearly articulated, since he wrote his earliest major poem, "Ode to the Setting Sun." Like much of his thought between 1894 and 1896, this theory of symbolism developed at least in part through conversations with Coventry Patmore, who Thompson declared often confirmed or extended many beliefs he had formulated independently: "yours is the conversation of a man who has trodden before me the way which for years I trod alone and often desperate, seeing no guiding parallel among modern poets to my aims and experience." In a notebook he recorded that this important friend "reverberated my idea with such and so many echoes that it returned to me greater than I gave it forth."[25]

In essence their shared theory of symbolism arises from a belief in the organic unity of all things in the universe and the Platonic principle that all in this physical world represents a higher reality. Thompson and Patmore more specifically held that the literary and religious symbols of various ages and cultures are related to each other, or that the symbols of one period or civilization may be said to prefigure those of another and to share their meanings. In 1894 Thompson had begun an essay on symbolism which, though never completed, expressed these ideas, suggesting that major symbols such as the sun or water implied many meanings that finally resolved themselves into one meaning.[26]

Thompson illustrates this idea in "The Mistress of Vision" by referring to Icarus and Perseus along with Christ and Noah. Moreover, he links Old Testament with New Testament episodes to demonstrate the symbolic parallels or prefigurations long familiar in Christian exegesis. Thompson specifically notes in the Lady's song that the vine

from which Noah wove his crown on Mount Ararat was the parent
stock of the crown of thorns from Golgotha that Christ wore to Cal-
vary. Thompson extends this prefigural relationship between Noah
and Christ to imply that any true poet, prefigured by the Lady singing about these biblical saviors, provides mankind access to salvation:
"from spear and thorn alone / May be grown / For the front of saint
or singer any divinizing twine."

Several other poems in the *Sight and Insight* section concern poetic
activity. "From the Night of Forebeing: An Ode After Easter," sent
to the Meynells in April 1894, contrasts the speaker's creative sterility ("Winter with me, alack! / Winter on every hand I find: / Soul,
brain, and pulses dead") with the fecund spring, which is symbolically associated with Christ's Resurrection. Thompson's evocation of
the Resurrection, reflected by Nature's orgiastic celebration, leads
him to anticipate renewed poetic power. God, the "Giver of
spring, / And song," "seest in me, so stripped and bare, / The lyric
secret waiting to be born."

In the elaborate "Orient Ode" (shown to Patmore by August
1895),[27] which like "From the Night of Forebeing" symbolizes Christ
as the life-giving sun, the poet shares his insight with the world: "I
can translate into mortal wire. . . / The heavenly harping
harmony, / Melodious, sealed, inaudible." In order to worship "In
such a song as hath within / A smouldering core of mystery," the
poet "pleads" that God will "Touch from yon altar my poor mouth's
desire, / And the relucent song take for thy sacred meeds!"

In "Contemplation," which immediately follows "The Mistress of
Vision," Thompson conveys a more positive picture of poetic energy,
for the speaker is not, as in "From the Night of Forebeing," excluded
from the positive rhythms of Nature. Like the idle, dozing pastoral
scene, he appears calm. The contemplative atmosphere of this poem
contrasts signficantly with the lethargic calm seen elsewhere in
Thompson's work, where imagery often suggests drug-induced ener-
vation. The apparent repose of both Nature and the poet here conceals
a dynamic, creative fermentation taking place unnoted. Even an inan-
imate object like a wall acquires life through subtle exchanges with
animate Nature:

> The wall to me has freshness like a scent,
> And takes half animate the air,

> Making one life with its green moss and stain;
> And life with all things seems too perfect blent
> For anything of life to be aware.

The interchange between wall and moss expresses one of the major themes of *Sight and Insight,* the organic unity of all creation. Thompson succinctly articulates the idea in "The Mistress of Vision" as one of the important truths the poet must learn to see:

> All things by immortal power,
> Near or far,
> Hiddenly
> To each other linkèd are,
> That thou canst not stir a flower
> Without troubling of a star.

"Contemplation" repeats the idea that observing these connections between all entities in the world requires more than mere sight: "From stones and poets you may know, / Nothing so active is, as that which least seems so." And as in "The Mistress of Vision," Thompson reinforces the importance of nonsensory insight by figuratively reorienting normal sensory powers. Here both the mute harmonious interchange among all objects in Nature and the creative activity occurring within the mind of the apparently unproductive poet are "heard" by the stars, which in turn "Shout to each other from the peaks of space." Thompson repeats the image in "New Year's Chimes." Imagining "the song the stars sing," he reiterates that all creation is interconnected: *"a million songs are as song of one."* "Contemplation," with its unusually detailed nature description, its emphasis on the organic unity and animation of all things in the world, and its view of the poet, calls to mind Wordsworth's characteristic verse, a similarity reinforced by Thompson's affirming a power immanent in the universe. In all this calm "Lurk untumultuous vortices of power."[28]

Like "The Mistress of Vision," "From the Night of Forebeing," and "Contemplation," the last of the twelve poems of the section, "Retrospect," describes the poet in relationship to the theme of sight and insight. The poet declares that most of his earlier verse has lacked true insight. He has "sung / Much song of matters vain, / And a heaven-sweetened tongue / Turned to unprofiting strain / Of vacant things." Occasionally, however, he has come near to proper vision. Consequently he anticipates "a wiser day" when he can sing "approvèd music" and "Fulfil more heavenly way." This lyric ends the *Sight and Insight* section with the poet resolving to suspend his singing until he achieves a stoic fortitude and spiritual insight: "Meantime the silent lip, / Meantime the climbing feet." This conclusion reiterates an important concept of the *Sight and Insight* section—that poetry is related to altruistic self-sacrifice and religious devotion. As "The Mistress of Vision" points out, the saint's coronal and poet's crown must be analogues to Christ's crown of thorns. Several poems throughout the section focus directly on religious purification, using the figure of a Lady to embody and teach the ideal. The Mistress of Vision has a more specifically religious counterpart in *"Assumpta Maria,"* a graceful lyric sent to Alice Meynell in September 1893 (published in *Merry England* in December) and closely patterned on the liturgical Office of the Assumption.[29] The poem is formulated as a celebratory hymn interesting in that Mary speaks most of it herself. Thompson acknowledges his indebtedness to the liturgy by describing himself as a "poor Thief of Song," a phrase by which his critics have referred to his penchant for echoing and borrowing from other writers.[30]

"The After Woman," which immediately follows *"Assumpta Maria,"* likewise describes a female embodiment of the ideal who by example may encourage the spiritual perfection of humanity. It prophesies a woman of the future who shall be an "after" woman in two senses. Coming after Eve, she will play an equivalent pivotal role in the history of man by instigating a second "Fall," one which reverses that wrought by Eve. Effecting man's return to divine favor, this woman envisioned by Thompson will be patterned "after" Mary, much as her song follows after *"Assumpta Maria."*

"The After Woman" uses explicitly sexual language in the manner of the Song of Songs, to which Thompson specifically refers. The speaker prophetically dreams of the as yet immature "Sister of the Canticle" becoming a woman, "for God grown marriageable." This appropriation of the language of connubial love to describe the metaphorical wedding of man and God shows the strong influence of Coventry Patmore, who developed this motif from the Old Testament throughout his major poetic works, *The Angel in the House* and *The Unknown Eros.* Thompson weaves related imagery into "From the Night of Forebeing," where Earth, "unchilded, widowed" by winter awaits the coming of the sun, symbol of the resurrected Christ: "Behold your bridegroom cometh in to you." Such imagery also recurs in "Orient Ode," which sustains the idea of a sensuous wedding between Christ and Earth.

Thompson develops the metaphoric association between sexual love and spiritual union most extensively in "Any Saint." He describes God or Christ as a lover wooing an unworthy mortal bride, who may become unjustifiably proud because of the lover's regard. The poem thus reminds readers of the individual's paradoxical identity as one who, though totally unworthy of the celestial bridegroom, is invested with merit by his affection. Mankind becomes "this narrow bed" in which "God's two worlds immense, / Of spirit and of sense, / Wed." This double nature of man is expressed in a series of resourceful metaphors. Man is a "Trope that itself not scans / Its huge significance," a "court" where "midge's hymn / Answers the seraphim," a "freak / Of heavenly hide-and-seek," a "dear nonentity," a "Cosmic metonymy," and a "Compost of Heaven and mire."

This metaphoric surprise, characteristic of Thompson at his best, is counterpointed in "Any Saint" (first published in *Merry England* in January 1894) with a happy choice of metaphor poignant for its simple familiarity. God's magnanimity is revealed through the image of the paltry "strength" by which man, like a child "forcing" an adult to stoop for a caress, wins God's affection: "Rise; for Heaven hath no frown / When thou to thee pluck'st down, / Strong Clod! / The neck of God." Such simple touches enliven other poems in *Sight and Insight*. "Grace of the Way," for example, another poem in which the Virgin provides insight into spiritual perfection, recasts the image: "Short arm needs man to reach to Heaven, / So ready is Heaven to stoop to him."

In "From the Night of Forebeing" much of Thompson's imagery is complex, requiring interpretive insight to probe beneath the visible surface. For instance, the title—taken from Sir Thomas Browne's phrase "In the chaos of preordination, and night of our forebeings"—perhaps implies that stoic acceptance is a necessary preliminary to true being: forebearance is fore-being. Yet even amid such verbal and metaphoric complexities Thompson employs a commonplace image to stress the need for every creature to strive for insight. Each celebrant of spring should search the season's spiritual significance: "Let even the slug-abed snail upon the thorn / Put forth a conscious horn!"

Some of the images in individual works of *Sight and Insight* accrue meaning by being echoed and extended in other poems of the group. Thompson's three substantial references to falcons illustrate this thematic amplification by metaphor. The poems draw on traditional symbolism of the falcon, which in classical antiquity was associated with the sun as a bird sacred to Apollo. More pertinent to Thompson's verse is the complex significance that the symbol acquired in Christian art. The wild falcon represents evil, whereas the domestic falcon represents the good man, especially the Christian convert, whose flight is wisely controlled by God. This Falconer not only orders the bird's flight by clipping its wings, but also commands it to safe haven in its mew for molting, a symbolic rebirth.[31]

In " 'By Reason of Thy Law' " the speaker, describing the lack of insight common to "the heart that knows its bitterness," depicts his own heart as a falcon to which God, the Falconer, has prohibited "food of all delight." Although this falconer "tames" the "haggard" heart "with fearful glooms," the stern trainer occasionally reveals his love with gestures ("sometimes comes a hand, sometimes a voice withal") that calm and enlighten the bird: "And she sits meek now, and expects the light." Vowing to withstand tribulation in an uncertain world, the speaker will endure with unabated vision:

> Nor all iniquity of the froward years
> Shall his inurèd wing make idly bate,
> Nor of the appointed quarry his staunch sight
> To lose observance quite.

In the following poem, "The Dread of Height," the poet describes the pain that insight may bring, for one who has truly glimpsed Heaven but not achieved it suffers Hell more acutely than another who remains ignorant of the alternative. An epigraph from John 9:41 suggests also the responsibility imposed by one's capacity to recognize the ideal: "If ye were blind, ye should have no sin: but now ye say: We see: your sin remaineth." Acknowledging that he can see the ideal, the speaker nonetheless fails to ascend to it because he knows that "low they fall whose fall is from the sky." He confesses, "I of height grown desperate / Surcease my wing." This failure to achieve lofty standards leaves him "Lower than man, for I dreamed higher." He clearly recognizes his "potential cousinship with mire"; conse-

quently "all my conquered skies do grow a hollow mock." This imagery of flight—or more precisely, of the failure to fly—culminates in
the speaker's wish to be either a falcon constrained from flight by
"hooded eye" and "jesses and restraint," or a falcon with a
"heart . . . native to high Heaven" and a winged ("accipitrine") will
to soar.

He rephrases his longing: to have the flesh of a merely ordinary man, content to remain confined and earthbound, like a molting
falcon ("in sickest time"), or else to have the "brave-fledging fervours
of the Saint, / Whose heavenly falcon-craft doth never taint."
Thompson concludes "From the Night of Forebeing" with another
extended falcon image. It describes the "firm" man who transcends
the adversities dealt in "Fortune's game":

> [His] falcon soul sits fast,
> And not intends her high sagacious tour
> Or ere the quarry sighted; who looks past
> To slow much sweet from little instant sour,
> And in the first does always see the last.

This passage specifically recalls the falcon's association in Christian art
with hope. Because its trainer veiled its eyes to preclude its striking
before the proper moment, the hooded falcon became widely used in
medieval emblem books to illustrate the motto *post tenebras spero lucem*
(I hope for light after darkness),[32] a phrase echoed in Thompson's epigraph taken from St. John and in his early manuscript title for the
poem, *"Lux in Tenebris."*[33] Thompson's symbolic falcon conveys one
of the important themes of *Sight and Insight,* a theme also prominent
in the works of Coventry Patmore and their common inspirations in
Christian and Platonic thought: true freedom consists of proper obedience to the highest law. Emotional strength and philosophical calm
arise from obedience to God the Falconer, who properly controls
man's vision and powers of flight.

Thompson rather carefully connected the dozen poems of *Sight and
Insight* by imagery, tone, and theme. Most are written in the irregular
ode form, with lines expanding and contracting to correspond to
thought and feeling, that he had employed earlier but increasingly
preferred and developed—as he developed his imagery and themes—
partly as a result of his fruitful exchanges with Patmore.[34] The group
of poems generally shows greater control and simplicity than *Sister
Songs* or the least successful works in *Poems.* Perhaps on the whole,

greater economy and concentration would intensify their artistic accomplishment—but generally the nineteenth-century aesthetic did not in this regard anticipate twentieth-century tastes. And unlike the volubility that characterized Thompson's conversation in his later years, his poetic verbosity is rarely inconsequential.

"Miscellaneous Odes" and "Miscellaneous Poems"

In addition to the odes of *Sight and Insight,* which are widely varied in length, rhyme scheme, and stanzaic pattern, *New Poems* includes a group of four miscellaneous odes, all of them interesting. The first is the splendid "Ode to the Setting Sun," Thompson's first mature poem. Although it had been published in *Merry England* in September 1889 (and is discussed before *Poems* in the preceding chapter), Thompson in December of 1895 submitted a revised version to the Meynells for their judgment on whether it should be included in the next collection.[35] The ode suits *New Poems* particularly well, for it develops many of the themes expressed in *Sight and Insight,* and, in focusing on the dual yet ultimately single identity of the sun as a symbol of both God and Apollo, it illustrates ideas about symbolism employed throughout the 1897 volume.

The effective concentration of metaphors in "Ode to the Setting Sun" is accentuated by contrast with the "Orient Ode" of *Sight and Insight,* which similarly praises God as symbolized by the sun. "Orient Ode," suggested by the liturgies of Holy Saturday and written soon after Easter 1895,[36] begins with a startling identification of the sun with the Host consumed at Holy Communion:

> Lo, in the sanctuaried East,
> Day, a dedicated priest
> In all his robes pontifical exprest,
> Lifteth slowly, lifteth sweetly,
> From out its Orient tabernacle drawn,
> Yon orbèd sacrament confest
> Which sprinkles benediction through the dawn.

The varied metaphors that follow this arresting analogy, while demonstrating the amplitude of Thompson's figurative inventiveness, lack the focus so forcefully concentrated in "Ode to the Setting Sun."

In keeping with the emphasis in the *Sight and Insight* section on the symbolic marriage between sun and earth, the last work in "Miscellaneous Odes" complements the first, in effect framing the section between sun and earth. "An Anthem of Earth" counterpoints the apostrophe to the sun in "Ode to the Setting Sun" by addressing the earth. It describes allegorically man's maturation during his life with this foster-mother.

Completed in October 1894 and published within a month in *Merry England,* the poem has inspired amazingly conflicting evaluations. Thompson's contemporaries called it, on the one hand, "the greatest rhapsody in English poetry" and Thompson's "most magnificent ode"—presumably surpassing "The Hound of Heaven"—and on the other hand, "a terrible poem without form and void."[37] The controversy continues among recent critics as well. Some judge that it fails as poetry but commands biographical interest. More disparagingly, John Reid finds it "stupefyingly ornate," marred by "verbosity, clouds of rhetoric and cosmic attitudinizing," and he patronizingly jests that "Here and there Thompson puts on his playboy-of-the-western-stars costume again."[38] Actually the ode is one of Thompson's finest achievements, less dazzling than "Ode to the Setting Sun," yet full of fine touches all neatly unified.

Thompson minimized the significance of "An Anthem of Earth" when he presented it to Alice Meynell "only as an exercise in blank verse," his "first serious attempt to handle that form." For this metrical exercise he had "transferred to it whole passages from my prose articles. So it is solely for your judgment on the metre that I send it."[39] Many lines do in fact translate into blank verse the prose of two early essays, "A Threnody of Birth," which Thompson had submitted for publication in 1890 or early 1891, and "Shelley," which he was writing in late 1889.[40] But rather than dismissing the thematic import of the poem, Thompson's acknowledging that it derives from his prose underscores his serious and continuing interest in the ideas, as does his specifically associating the poem with the blank verse in the later plays of his revered Shakespeare.[41]

By separating human experience into seven stages, ranging from "nescientness" to a physical death that is actually spiritual renewal, Thompson works a variation on the motif of the Seven Ages of Man familiar from medieval and Renaissance literature, and concisely catalogued in secular terms by the "All the world's a stage" speech in Shakespeare's *As You Like It.* Thompson's religious theme that death constitutes release from pain echoes the medieval Christian *Sic transit mundi* tradition.

A "Proemion" addressed to Earth relates the anthem to the themes of *Sight and Insight;* dominant olfactory imagery establishes the poet's concern with attaining not superficial understanding but true vision. Despite his "custom-dulled perceivingness," he discerns in the "fume of its circumfluous self" the essential nature of even a "cold-seeming stone." Although he recognizes true essence, the poet's artistic powers are failing: "in all too late and frozen a day / I come in rearward of the throats of song, / Unto the deaf sense of the agèd year." Seen in terms of the falcon imagery of *Sight and Insight,* he is but a "poet with sick pinion." Not merely a personal lament over waning poetic inspiration, as biographers tend to read it, this prologue illustrates in the speaker himself the diminishment of joy and stamina that becomes the topic of the poem proper.

The body of the anthem recounts the phases of human experience in a series of imaginative metaphors. In childhood, for example, during which man dwelt "in a little joy," the Earth indulged him like her petted offspring. The boy demanded that his mother join his play, as he "brake through thy doors of sunset, / Ran before the hooves of sunrise." But eventually the poet's recollections darken considerably, as the variations on clothing imagery suggest. Whereas the joyful child wore Earth's "insignia" carelessly, the young man passing to "a little thought" sees fleshly garb as "hasty tarnished piecings negligent, / Snippets and waste / From old ancestral wearings, / That have seen sorrier usage." In such garb "Our souls go out at elbows."

Thompson suggests man's concern with temporalia not only through this clothing metaphor, but also through a cluster of housing images. Despite man's proximity to the celestial (he "Sifts in his hands the stars, weighs them as gold-dust"), he inherits only "patrimony of a little mould, / And entail of four planks." His final physical residence is a grave, "To stall the grey-rat, and the carrion-worm / Statelily lodge."

This "little knowledge" demands a stoic resilience experienced in the next phase of life, described as "a little strength." Despite his disheartened sense that his poetic inspiration is dwindling ("I the Orient never more shall feel / Break like a clash of cymbals, and my heart / Clang through my shaken body like a gong"), the speaker must endure "With wide eyes calm upon the whole of things."

This fortitude brings man to the vantage point of modest wisdom, "a little sight," which, though not proving the validity of religious hope, at least enables him to resist the nihilistic teachings of mere reason. Refusing to declare that "There's nought beyond," he also refuses to accept the narrow coffin as his permanent dwelling, extending the housing metaphor from the preceding stanza. Unable to explore "those dim catacombs, / Where the rat memory does its burrows make," he can hardly predict what habitation awaits beyond the grave:

> Who the chart shall draw
> Of the strange courts and vaulty labyrinths,
> The spacious tenements and wide pleasances,
> Innumerable corridors far-withdrawn,
> Where I wander darkling, of myself?

He attempts with his "wise foot-rule" to measure the "walls o' the world." Judging it a *"goodly house, but something ancient,"* he must look to a *"Master"* for fuller knowledge.

This stanza stressing the limitations of human wisdom criticizes the pretensions of science to explode religious tenets. Science, an "old noser in its prideful straw," works "with anatomising scalpel." With demoralizing rationale that prefers to discover chemical and mechanical explanations for decay rather than to hope for growth, science sees "Life in putridity, vigour in decay" and judges "admirable the manner of our corruption / As of our health." Without intending to do so, this clinically dispassionate satisfaction with decay and death supports the religious vision of spiritual rebirth, for Christianity interprets "decay" as a stage toward "vigour" and "corruption" as the preliminary to "health."

In the sixth stage of existence, "in a little dust," man inhabits "a haunted tenement, / Peopled from barrows and outworn ossuaries." Besides the dwelling metaphor, this stanza also picks up from the preceding one the role of scientific thought. Nearing his own death, the individual recognizes Nature's history of extinguishing entire species. Though strikingly similar to Tennyson's treatment of the theme in *In Memoriam* (55–56), Thompson's imagery and language becomes characteristically hyperbolic when he considers human extinction:

> Thou hast devoured mammoth and mastodon,
> And many a floating bank of fangs,
> The scaly scourges of thy primal brine,

And the tower-crested plesiosaure.
Thou fill'st thy mouth with nations, gorgest slow
On purple aeons of kings; man's hulking towers
Are carcase for thee. . . .

The final stanza of "An Anthem of Earth" extols the release man shall find "in a little peace." The phrase, anticipating permanent respite from care, ironically points up the literal appropriateness of the word "little" for describing the phases of life that seemed so important to the man living them. Hardly the cowardly death wish that recent biographers have interpreted it to be,[42] this conclusion fits into a long tradition of somber celebrations of man's release from the duress of this world into the peace of the next, the "Sentence . . . of life" finally relieved by "commutation / Petitioning into death."

Critics who have thought the title incongruous because the poem discusses not earth but man's experience miss the point that the anthem assesses the ignorance and sorrow of man *as* earth, as a son of God who temporarily dwells in flesh as the foster-child of Earth. The final lines assert in deceptively quiet language man's triumph over his confinement in clay, to be achieved by consigning his body to clay. As the speaker tells Earth, "my cell is set / Here in thy bosom; my little trouble is ended / In a little peace."

Although it lacks the rhythmical intensity of "The Hound of Heaven" or the extravagant surprises of other works and, like most of his poetry, occasionally uses intrusive neologisms or archaisms, "An Anthem of Earth" is one of Thompson's finest poems. It offers language enriched by multiple connotations;[43] abundantly resourceful images which are often purposely echoed and patterned; and especially effective use of stark metaphors (reminiscent of seventeenth-century Metaphysical poets) which are simultaneously cerebral and emotional.

The characterizations in "An Anthem of Earth" of science as an "old noser in its prideful straw" and of Nature ruthlessly destroying entire species raises the issue of Thompson's view of the apparent conflict, so traumatic for the nineteenth century, between scientific analysis and religious faith. Having been more preoccupied with poetry and philosophy than with science during his days in medical school, Thompson used scientific perceptions in imaginative ways throughout his verse. The passage in his "Shelley" essay that developed into the portrayal of science in "An Anthem of Earth" suggests the importance of scientific scrutiny as a means of cultivating true insight, for science demands that man look beyond the surface of things: "amidst mate-

rial nature, where our dull eyes see only ruin, the finer eye of science
has discovered life in putridity and vigour in decay, seeing dissolution
even and disintegration, which in the mouth of man symbolize disor-
der, to be in the works of God undeviating order, and the manner of
our corruption to be no less wonderful than the manner of our
health."[44] The prose passage states directly what the poem suggests
obliquely—the role of science in pointing the way to higher truth.

Elsewhere in *New Poems* Thompson suggests the complementary relationship between scientific analysis and religious as well as imaginative interpretations of creation. "A Dead Astronomer," one of the
"Miscellaneous Poems," commemorates the death of a priest who was
also an astronomer. After all his preoccupation with scientific stargaz-
ing, the astronomer discovered the "fairest Star of all," Mary, when
he dropped his telescope ("thy hand its tube let fall") and metaphorically became a star himself. When Thompson sent the poem to Wilfrid Meynell in February 1890, he described it as but "a few fugitive
verses," and later he wrote, "I meant the thing merely for a pretty,
gracefully turned fancy; what the Elizabethans would have called an
excellent conceit." But he also recognized, after it appeared in *Merry
England* in April 1890, that it was his first poem to excite "any praise
from Catholic outsiders," or readers beyond the literary circle associated with the Meynells.[45]

The third of the "Miscellaneous Odes," "Against Urania," reminds
us that Thompson concerned himself less with science than with
myth and poetry. But the figure of Urania actually joins the three,
for in classical mythology she was the muse of astronomy, icono-
graphically represented by a globe and pair of compasses, and in Renaissance literature she became the muse of poetry—mistress of the
stars, patroness of great men, and termed by Milton the sister of eternal wisdom. Thompson's brief ode expresses the frustration of a lover
of this poetic muse, who proves to be a much more willful and elusive
object of devotion than mortal women. The ode calls to mind a tradition of complaints by the poet against an unresponsive muse, and like
many such poems it is richly ironic insofar as the description of poetic
sterility is itself a poetic tour de force of intricately patterned, densely
rhyming lines.

Like the two framing poems of "Miscellaneous Odes," "Against
Urania" and the second work in the section, "A Captain of Song,"
extend the themes of *Sight and Insight*. Between the first and last odes
addressed to sun and earth, which throughout the volume symbolize

God and man, the two middle poems explore the poet's difficulty in mediating between transcendent truth and human understanding. "Against Urania" expresses the problem of deriving inspiration from a divine source that remains aloof and uncommunicative, whereas "A Captain of Song" implies the gap between a poet and uncomprehending readers.

"A Captain of Song" is important biographically as Thompson's tribute to his uniquely important friend, Coventry Patmore, who in a sense had filled the role of his personal muse. Although Thompson sent the poem in manuscript to Patmore in September 1895, it was first published in the *Athenaeum* on 5 December 1896, as an obituary notice of the older poet's death in late November. Inspired, as the headnote indicates, by "a portrait of Coventry Patmore by J. S. Sargent," the poem effectively conveys the stern, even haughty demeanor of the painting, which caused Patmore to protest "I am not . . . that Dantesque being, which you and Sargent make me out to be."[46] In part, this "Dantesque" aspect, incorporating the idea that a poet suffers beyond the limits of ordinary mortals, may characterize not so much Patmore individually as the Poet generically. This implication reverberates in the challenging tone of the ode's address to readers, which suggests that they can scarcely appreciate the nature or intensity of the poet's experience.

One other detail indicates that the poem depicts not merely Patmore but the Poet. Thompson contrasts Patmore's life with that of "comfortable men," those who, like Matthew Arnold's Philistines, remain smugly unaware of the beauty and the pain known by the sensitive artist who has walked "the ways of dreadful greatness." Years later (1905) Thompson used similar vocabulary to describe his own life as one mostly lived "aside from the ways of 'comfortable men,' "[47] the ordinary beings who in the ode to Patmore speak words "accursed" and "abhorred" by the true Poet. Thompson also discussed in prose the typical reader's inability to comprehend such poetry as Patmore's mystical work, *The Unknown Eros*. An unpublished manuscript parodies Shakespeare's unimaginative literalist Rosencrantz to describe the Victorian Philistine, a lover of suet-pudding, as "Puddencrantz."[48]

The experience of the Poet provides a topic for several of the "Miscellaneous Poems." "Field-Flower: a Phantasy" implies that on a smaller scale, the poet's creativity parallels God's. But the poet, who begins to fashion "a flaw of pain" and "A hap of skiey pleasure" into a poem that "mingled them in measure," learns instead to study the "meaning" of the flower fashioned by God. He will sing again only when he can communicate the wisdom of such simple things to mankind. Like many in the group of "Miscellaneous Poems," this lyric sings in brief, lilting lines and simple rhyme scheme. It offers a quaint image of the flower speaking eloquently of divine craftsmanship: "Garrulous of the eyes of God / To all the breezes near it; / Musical of the mouth of God / To all had eyes to hear it."

"The Cloud's Swan-Song" presents a more melancholy view of the poet, but also shows him learning a poignant and uplifting lesson from Nature. The poet here has lost inspiration: "Like grey clouds one by one my songs upsoar / Over my soul's cold peaks; and one by one / They loose their little rain, and are no more." His sense of the correspondence between the desolate landscape and his own psychological and artistic condition soon falters, however, when a passing cloud demonstrates his weakness. The cloud illustrates how to withstand adversity: it "did not disdain / To sit in shadow and oblivious cold." Moreover, its dissolution teaches the speaker to accept mutability, to "fit myself to change with virtue ever new."

This theme of man's learning from the example of Nature permeates the "Miscellaneous Poems." The speaker in "To the Sinking Sun," echoing the dejection initially seen in "The Cloud's Swan-Song," contrasts himself with the sun, who "graciously" wears "the yoke / Of use that does not fail," while the man cannot endure the daily repetition of his pain: "Immutability mutable / Burthens my spirit and the skies." The speaker in "Grief's Harmonics" similarly laments unrelieved griefs of old, but at the evening hour "when all old dead things seem most dead, / And their death . . . most undying," he anticipates the advent of new woe, "an unborn calamity, / Ere its due time to be delivered." He recognizes that "in new pang old pang's incarnated."

In other "Miscellaneous Poems" contemplating some aspect of Nature makes the speaker aware of the variety, beauty, and goodness of God's creation. Instead of recording the somber ruminations of careworn speakers, these works depict the cheerful queries of innocents. "To a Snow-Flake" (first published in a much longer version, "A Hymn to Snow," in the February 1891 issue of *Merry England*) questions "What heart could have thought" the "filigree petal" from "argentine vapour." In feminine rhymes and lilting dimeter lines of preponderantly lightly accented syllables, it conjures a delightful image of God as a delicate silversmith. "A Question" also suggests God's deft craftsmanship by asking a tiny bird, a "poet of the blue," how it views man. The work becomes a whimsical lesson in perspective as the poet, declaring that "small things, ah, wee things, / Are the poets all," realizes that to angels he must seem as tiny as the bird seems to him. He recognizes, too, his own limited insight: "Alack! you tall angels, / I can't think so high! / I can't think what it feels like / Not to be I." The innocent, lighthearted tone of these last two poems continues in "A May Burden," a conscious imitation of medieval and Renaissance celebrations of spring,[49] which ends by jocularly refusing to describe the "blossom" that grows from blissful kisses in "wanton May." "July Fugitive," which wonders what has become of the happy month, sounds a gay note even while implying more troubling issues beneath the surface.

The most memorable of the happier "Miscellaneous Poems" is *"Ex Ore Infantium,"* first published in *Merry England* in May 1893 and more commonly known as "Little Jesus."[50] Formulated as a young child's asking Jesus questions about His own childhood, the poem calls to mind the language of naive speakers in Blake's *Songs of Innocence.* But Thompson's lyric has none of the irony implicit in Blake's antithesis between the fresh view of his innocent speakers and the grim actualities of the world. *"Ex Ore Infantium"* (the title alluding to Psalm 8:3) translates the mystery of the Incarnation into an apparently natural event remarkable for its simplicity: "Little Jesus, wast Thou shy / Once, and just so small as I? / And what did it feel like to be / Out of Heaven, and just like me?" The child's curiosity about Christ's life as a human being not only illustrates his unspoiled simplicity and naive trust that others' experiences must resemble his own, but also reveals his intuitive understanding of the contrast between celestial purity and mortal taint: "And did Thy Mother let Thee spoil / Thy robes, with playing on *our* soil?" With Christ the beloved Son as man's intermediary, the paternal God of this charming poem seems infinitely accessible.

In contrast, two lyrics among the "Miscellaneous Poems" underscore the melancholy side of human passion. In the pleasantly understated "Nocturne," "Nothing is, this sweet night, / But doth couch and wake / For its love's sake." Only the frustrated speaker, denied love's kiss, passes the night in pain. *"Memorat Memoria,"* perhaps recalling Thompson's experience with the young prostitute in London, hints of agonizing memories of a past love who was both pure and

polluted: "your awful self is embalmed in the fragrant self I knew."
The poem evokes a complex relationship. He feels both guilty for the
way he treated her and revolted by her contaminated beauty: "You
have made a thing of innocence as shameful as a sin, / I shall never
feel a girl's soft arms without horror of the skin."

"Miscellaneous Poems" closes with a group of six Shakespearean
sonnets and two poetic translations from Victor Hugo's *Feuilles d'Au-
tomne*. Though generally competent, the sonnets pale beside the great
models Thompson obviously followed. The most interesting,
"Hermes," begins dramatically and concisely suggests symbolic
aspects of the gods' messenger. Thompson's insistence that the Hugo
translations remain in *New Poems* even if other material had to be cut
scarcely seems justified by their mediocrity, but they illustrate
his principle, stated in an 1899 review, that a translator, after
"catching . . . something sympathetic" to his own spirit in the original, should make the translation "verily his own."[51]

The group of "Miscellaneous Poems" exhibits a conciseness and directness not often found in Thompson's odes and poetic sequences.
Distinguished like his longer works by abundant, striking metaphors,
the short poems offer a welcome naturalness and a gift for phrasing
sometimes memorable for its simplicity. But the entire volume of
New Poems, even the allegorical "Mistress of Vision" and the elaborate
"Ode to the Setting Sun" and "An Anthem of Earth," is more controlled, less given to freakish flights or verbal extravagance than his
earlier work. Thompson called attention to this restraint in a note he
originally intended to include in the volume: "Of words I have coined
or revived I have judged fit to retain but few; and not more than two
or three will be found in this book. I shall also be found, I hope, to
have modified much the excessive loading both of diction and imagery
which disfigured my former work."[52]

Although the language of *New Poems* may be more eccentric than
Thompson realized, this last collection published in his lifetime deserves to be more widely known. It offers richly varied works, ranging from the exuberantly decorative "Ode to the Setting Sun" to the
touchingly simple *"Ex Ore Infantium."* The poems show a commendable range of tone and emotion. John Walsh observes that in the 1897
volume "it was not the Thompson of old that came to life, the soaring, prodigally gifted image-maker. The old cosmic exuberance had
faded, in fact had been deliberately smothered, and in its place was a
sober striving after new levels of mystical thought, and a deliberate

effort to achieve a calmer, quieter, sparer expression." And Walsh finally judges, "he was not one whose genius could be made to submit to conscious control in any great degree, and if he succeeded in his quest for conscious significance he did so at the cost of song."[53] Admittedly, the verse of *New Poems* does not sing so affectingly as the sometimes incantatory rhythms of "The Hound of Heaven"; nevertheless, Thompson's jewels of imagery often shine more brightly for their simpler settings in *New Poems*.

Contemporary critical reception was mixed. Thompson felt that the earliest reviews were almost uniformly hostile, so much so that in May 1897, when the volume appeared, he gratefully thanked William Archer for showing "a courage, an independence, a chivalry" in making "a gallant last stand" by reviewing the book positively.[54] After what he termed "the organized violence with which it was assailed on its first appearance," however, Thompson had to acknowledge by early summer that "It has gone rather better as regards reviews than I expected." *New Poems* sold 350 copies in the first week after publication and was chosen by the *Morning Post* (30 December 1897) as the best volume of poetry released that year.[55]

Shortly after he had sent the manuscript to the publisher, Thompson had revealed to Alice Meynell that "The whole book I look back to as a bad dream, so unexampled in my previous experience was the labour I bestowed on it."[56] In the same month, June 1896, he confessed to Coventry Patmore that "This will certainly be my last volume for at any rate a few years, possibly altogether, unless my bodily decline is stayed."[57] Yet within two months Thompson seems to have begun again to write verse described by John Walsh as "full of a youthful ardor."[58]

Chapter Four

Uncollected, Posthumously Published, and Unpublished Poetry

Thompson's romantic attachment to Katie King beginning in the summer of 1896 revived his poetic energy, and between that time and the beginning of 1900 he wrote a great deal of new verse. All but one of the works addressed to Katie King remained unpublished until after his death; some remain unprinted even today. In addition to these poems written after 1896, Thompson at his death left a large number of works that had never been gathered into books. Of almost three hundred poems that have now been identified and published in some form, only about one-third appeared in his lifetime. Three significant posthumous collections more than doubled the canon known at the time of his death, and biographies have made available still other works, often only in fragments.[1]

Establishing texts for Thompson's verse is particularly complicated. Discrepancies exist between versions published in periodicals and apparently final copies in the author's hand, and in at least one instance during the poet's life Wilfrid Meynell deleted a large section before passing a poetry manuscript along to the printer.[2] Several unpublished poems exist in more than one version or in drafts that leave a choice of readings unresolved. And some finished poems have been withheld from publication by editors who may have thought they were following the poet's wishes.

The Unknown Poet

In 1897, the year of his last poetry collection, Thompson himself argued against reviving works that a poet had chosen not to print. Reviewing a posthumous edition of Tennyson's poems, which included works the Laureate had refused to print, Thompson declared that their publication only demonstrated "how little we lose, how much we gain" by a poet's "self-limitation." The lesson should "impress upon young poets the necessity of using like self-denial."[3] But circumstances bearing on the publication of Thompson's own poetry, even during his lifetime, may encourage twentieth-century readers to resurrect poems that he never published. Factors other than his critical judgment clearly influenced his "self-denial."

From the beginning of his writing career Thompson's publication was heavily influenced by the tastes of his literary advisors, the Meynells, but even more by the nature of the audience for the journals that were his principal outlets.[4] Most of Thompson's poetry first appeared in publications aimed at Catholic readers, and the fact that he never achieved a substantially wider, nondenominational audience troubled him. Considerations of propriety as much as religion influenced the Meynells' recommendations. Because they wanted to protect their friend and protégé from lurid gossip about his drug addiction and life in the streets, they counseled the poet to suppress work that reflected that experience. In the special case of the love poems to Katie King discretion also urged withholding works that might embarrass the young woman who had refused Thompson and soon married another.

Thompson's letters record occasional disputes with the Meynells about the quality of his work. Although he sometimes defended his word choice, he frequently accepted their suggestions for altering his poetry, even to the extent of withdrawing a poem from a collection about to go to press.[5]

An important argument for printing previously neglected texts is that Thompson in fact planned to publish another collection of poetry. In January 1898 he wrote his publisher Arthur Doubleday that he had "material for a thin volume" and could produce a collection quickly: "A happy fit might carry me through in three; but if the Muse were unwilling, it might take six months."[6] The letter mentions poems he might include, and a notebook lists other possibilities. He also chose a title, *First Fruits and Aftermath*, that suggests the volume might have included some older uncollected or unpublished work. He particularly intended to print some of the poetry addressed to Katie King. She returned the copies he had sent her in order to facilitate his preparing a manuscript for the press.[7]

But Thompson's hopes for the new collection seem to have vanished with his dream of a future with Katie, as he indicated to Wil-

frid Meynell when he mentioned the aborted publishing plans in
connection with Katie's announcement of her forthcoming marriage:
"The terrible blow of the New Year put an end to that project."[8] Yet
even in the days of darkest despair which followed, when he expected
to surrender to addiction and return to the streets, he derived comfort
from the thought that his poems to Katie might be published.

Without Wilfrid Meynell, Thompson would probably never have
become known. Certainly without his friendship, financial assistance,
and supervision of Thompson's medical problems, the poet would
never have written so much. But without Meynell's strong influence
over what was published and the form it took, Thompson might to-
day be known as a substantially different poet. The posthumously
published and unpublished material shows a range of subject matter,
tone, and technical achievement that might have commended the
work to a wider audience than Thompson has so far enjoyed. Some
works reveal incisive irony, dark humor, spareness of expression, and
concentrated symbolism—a modernity not seen in the familiar canon
or appreciated by those who have commented on his work. Though
too large to be more than briefly surveyed here, the body of uncollected and unpublished poetry reveals intriguing and little-known
faces of Thompson.

The poems range from sober religious odes to graceful love sonnets
to bumptious satire. Thompson captured contemporary life in a vivid,
concise evocation of a train as "a pauseless, black Necessity," in a
satire of the average citizen as "Brown, from the loins of Philistines,"
and in doggerel on the Boer War.[9] He looked to the romantic past
in imitations of medieval ballads and chansons, and to the future in
prophetic verse in biblical rhetoric. He translated Horace and Victor
Hugo. He practiced the ornate and flowery style characteristic of his
earliest verse, and he experimented with a condensed and symbolic
idiom. Several brief pieces might be described as forerunners of the
early twentieth-century Imagist movement.[10]

Many of these poems are admittedly trivial, even though Thompson sometimes tried to bring out deeper meanings in overtly slight
matter. In "Cricket Verses," for example, sometimes called "At
Lord's" (*Poems*, 1:174), Thompson attempted to suggest the pathos of
mutability by evoking his favorite cricket players from the past.[11] In
an equally trivial but amusing verse manuscript he described his un-
successful attempt to help the Meynells prepare their journals:
"biting / My pencil, inviting / Inspiration and plighting / My hair
into elf-locks most wild, and affrighting."[12]

Other poems initially published in *Merry England* but not reprinted in book form are obviously derivative. "Song of the Hours" (*Poems,* 1:204), for example, published in *Merry England* in January 1890 and patently derived from the chorus of the Hours in Shelley's *Prometheus Unbound,* pays handsome tribute to Shelley's influence by employing the echoes of his prosody and Platonism to artful ends. Like most of Thompson's early works, it boasts abundant, often felicitous imagery (dreams, for instance, described as bees that feed on "the blossoms of day" and "swarm to the slumbers / That cell the hive of the dark"). Likewise indebted to Shelley and his concept of spiritual permanence is "*Buona Notte*" (*Poems,* 1:169), a lyric in which Thompson imagines the spirit of the dead Shelley replying to a letter that Jane Williams actually wrote him before his drowning. Although Thompson indicated that he wanted to publish "*Buona Notte,*" it remained unprinted until it appeared in the *Athenaeum* in July 1909.

While Alice Meynell thought "*Buona Notte*" a "little masterpiece," Wilfrid dismissed another, much better, early poem as seeming too derivative.[13] When Meynell printed "Daphne" (*Poems,* 1:176) in the May 1890 issue of *Merry England,* Thompson expressed surprise, for the editor had complained that it too much resembled a work by Elizabeth Barrett Browning.[14] Yet "Daphne" is one of Thompson's most original and effective poems on the subject of poetry. It uses the myth of Daphne and Apollo, the reluctant lady fleeing the god's amorous overtures, as a richly ironic metaphor to represent the conflict within the poet, who is both artist and man. By forcing Daphne's metamorphosis into the laurel tree, which becomes the emblem of poetic accomplishment, Apollo denies himself the mortal woman he desired. Apollo's "love-banning love . . . barks the man about with the poet, / And muffles his heart of mortality!" Unified by its dominant metaphor and enriched by internal rhyme, repetition, and feminine rhythms, the poem is dry, sometimes subtly comic, as in the concluding observation that poetic fame does not essentially distinguish a dead Keats from any "Hob, Dick, Marian, and Margery." Employing *barks* and *throes* as verbs, for example ("She throes in his arms to a laurel-tree"), Thompson, who was maligned by his contemporaries for his neologisms and archaisms, reveals the verbal invention that has so much recommended Gerard Manley Hopkins to the twentieth century.

Meynell may have preferred the slight but derivative "*Buona Notte*" to the more resourceful "Daphne" partly because he admired Thompson's discretion in handling the relationship between Shelley and his

last extramarital interest. Meynell probably counseled Thompson to
suppress several interesting works because they revealed unsavory details of the poet's own life. Such a work is "The Nightmare of the
Witch-Babies," a substantial piece of 144 lines arranged in twelve
stanzas. It depicts in ghoulish allegorical symbolism his relationship
to the prostitute who rescued him from the streets. Though it was
among the first pieces Thompson ever sent to Wilfrid Meynell, it was
one of the "witch-opium poems" Alice Meynell detested and the
Meynells chose to suppress. [15]

Besides its obvious biographical interest, the poem has substantial
artistic appeal. Describing the destruction of idealism by the horrors
of the city, Thompson masterfully grafts surrealistic symbolism onto
the conventions of medieval romance and allegory and produces a devastating indictment of moral corruption. In a London described as
"the land / Where the silence feels alone . . . the land / Of the Bare
Shank-Bone," a "lusty knight" rides into a "rotten mist" to find "a
maiden / Fairest fair," of "dreaming eyes" and "misty hair." But the
fair damsel reflects the decadence of her surroundings, a landscape of
"greasy soil" in which "Red bubbles oozed and stood; / Till it grew
a putrid slime." Like the shape-shifters of medieval romance, she
"Grew laidly old and dire, / Was the demon-ridden witch, / And the
consort of Hell-fire." With her the knight begets a "babe / Of
bloated youth," from whom evil breaks forth, a sickening ooze released in a nightmarish parody of a birth from a "paunch a-swollen"
which is "rent / Like a brasten drum." This ooze eventually suffocates
the knight.

The symbolic details of the transformation of beauty and innocence
into "two witch-babies" who live in "the Strand / Of the Dead Men's
Groan" achieve a horrible intensity made even more macabre by a refrain of mocking demonic laughter. The simple stanzaic pattern and
refrain, as well as the fairy-tale motifs, ironically emphasize the gap
between the actualities of street life and the beauty of romance.

Imagery from this tale of the witch-babies figures in another suppressed poem written during Thompson's vagrancy in London and
copied into a Notebook of Early Poems which he probably prepared
when Meynell first asked to see what else he had written. In "The
Owl," the nocturnal bird, with "eyes that bicker and gleam," is the
"witch of the cauldron of sleep" who, like the disembodied demonic
refrain in "Nightmare of the Witch-Babies," laughs balefully as she
stirs up a brew of horror—toads and serpents of materialism and lust,

"Adders of longing and fanged regrets," and living nightmares for the "sleep that sleepeth not."[16]

The unpublished poems from his period of dereliction occasionally reveal a modernist Thompson—pessimistic, darkly ironic, cryptically symbolic. Moreover, evidence of the suppression of a later prose manuscript in which Thompson described his own experiences as a vagrant indicates that his literary advisors most likely counseled him to avoid treating a topic that might have produced his most compelling verse.[17] At least one unpublished fragment suggests that he could describe life among London vagrants with disturbingly concrete, dispassionately realistic detail.[18]

The Poet of Human Love

Unlike the poems that never reached print because they revealed the underside of life, a substantial number of poems may have remained unpublished in Thompson's life initially because the poet and his editors observed polite discretion regarding his romantic liaisons. Both propriety and reticence probably kept *"Une Fille de Joie"* (*MHW*, 43) out of print. This sonnet, also copied into the Notebook of Early Poems, may well reflect Thompson's sense of guilt over leaving his friend the prostitute so that he could return to respectability and begin his poetic career. Bitingly ironic, it purports to denounce a fallen woman while absolving the speaker of his share in the harlot's guilt: "while I, chaste I, / In cheap immaculateness avert mine eye." Perhaps influenced by Dante Gabriel Rossetti's "Jenny," the poem acridly condemns smug materialism and the hypocrisy of facile moral judgments. To intensify emotion Thompson varies the Petrarchan sonnet form by concluding with a couplet, which echoes the four a-rhymes of the octave, to make the last line recall the first: "The gates of Hell have shut her in alive."

An unpublished poem entitled "Wild-Flower," earlier called *"A la Marguerite,"* records quite different feelings probably associated with Maggie Brien, whose triviality Thompson depicted in the sequence *A Narrow Vessel.* Lacking the variety of artistic devices and the occasional wit and modulations of tone that soften the criticisms of the girl in that sequence, the quatrains of "Wild-Flower" appraise shallowness with uncompromising bluntness.[19]

The later love poems to Katie King were probably withheld in Thompson's lifetime partly because the Meynells advocated sparing the young bride embarrassment. But the depth of feeling that kept the works out of print is precisely what distinguishes them from his other love poetry. The nature of the full body of poems addressed to Katie King remains to be established by careful editing. Only one poem inspired by the relationship appeared during Thompson's life. Entitled "An Arab Love-Song" (Poems, 1:168) and published in the Dome in January 1899, this fine lyric exudes an Eastern ambience probably suggested to Thompson by his visit to the estate of the Meynells' friend Wilfrid Blunt, a wealthy Arabic enthusiast. In three brief stanzas the poem economically but vividly evokes this foreign atmosphere, beginning with the speaker's description of clouds as the "hunchèd camels of the night." The wooer beseeches his beloved to leave her family: "what needest thou with thy tribe's black tents / Who hast the red pavilion of my heart?"[20]

The other love poems written between mid-1896 and the beginning of 1900, when Katie announced her engagement to another man—and when Thompson virtually stopped writing verse—have never been fully identified or adequately edited. A substantial number of lyrics probably dating from this period reflect intense emotions in a subdued manner quite unlike the flamboyant, self-consciously artful love sequences addressed to Alice Meynell. At times these later verses exalt the beloved lady effusively, as in a long poem of eighteen eleven-line stanzas, which exists only in manuscript, "Nocturnes of My Friend."[21] Thompson later judged this poem a "real failure" because it eulogized the lady in the manner of Love in Dian's Lap. Yet even in this work the unadorned poignancy characteristic of other poems to Katie King occasionally glints. Most of the lyrics drop the courtly conventions of the earlier sequence. Instead of focusing on worship, which must necessarily remain spiritual because the speaker is unworthy of the idealized lady, the later poems describe the anxieties of a lover who yearns for a reciprocal and fully human relationship with a special woman.

Several lyrics record the speaker's joyful discovery of wordless communion with his love. An unpublished poem, probably dating from the summer of 1896, recognizes that the two of them "became / A single effluence in a double frame, / One being distinct in two, and yet the same."[22] Such passages are thrown into relief by Thompson's musings in the undated prose work "Out of the House of Bondage" that no true communion can exist, even between lovers.[23] Many of the lyrics to Katie King refute a belief in individual isolation, insisting that once two people have established "inward converse," their bond persists despite separation. An unpublished poem of forty lines entitled "A Lost Friend," dated 27 July 1896, and probably written on the day Thompson arrived in Pantasaph (having been sent away from London against his will at the request of Katie's mother), reveals the pain of parting. Though sentimental, the poem feelingly describes his "fall" from isolation to love:

> From height, and cold, and mist I fell,
> With furlèd wing; and on my way
> What waited one, and what befell—
> The silence at Song's heart can only say.

To this plaint of longing, Thompson in the manuscript appended three couplets, dated 31 July, which affirm "She hath found out a way / That we in severance are bound."[24] Moreover, losing this lady "Makes one more rich than gain of any else!" Yet the pain of separation permeates the love lyrics. In "Absence" (*Poems*, 1:178–79) the lover dreads the passing of summer's sweets and of the precious friendship. "The Solemn Voice" (*MHW*, 25) describes the speaker's attempt to subdue the pain of lost love, to "Stand like a lonely tower / Amidst the grim lean life which works thee wrong," to "teach Love himself / To dread the shaking of the whip, / And fold his lovely passionate wings."

Some of these touching lyrics appear in a manuscript notebook containing sonnets collectively entitled *Ad Amicam* (To a Friend). It seems clear that Thompson viewed these poems as a sequence, but the exact makeup of the series is uncertain. The *Ad Amicam* notebook, into which he probably copied poems that he had sent individually to Katie as he wrote them, contains both sonnets and varied lyrics. The publishing history of poems in the notebook has obscured connections between them.

For example, a simple lyric probably written in the late summer of 1896, "To a Wind" (*MHW*, 31), expresses the desire of the speaker separated from his beloved to be caressed by breezes that have "blown / Across her fragrant mouth!" The quatrains were originally intended for the *Ad Amicam* series, as were several other lyrics of varying form. But *Ad Amicam*, as it was first published by Wilfrid Meynell, comprised only five sonnets. In 1957 Terence Connolly published seven additional sonnets related by content and style to the *Ad*

Amicam works. Three of these sonnets were gathered in "A Poetic Sequence" with another lyric, not a sonnet, in an arrangement that Connolly attributed to Thompson. These four poems appear in the *Ad Amicam* notebook. Another two of the sonnets that resemble *Ad Amicam,* though found in separate pencil manuscripts rather than in the notebook, Connolly printed in a section called "Sonnets." To complicate matters further, two additional sonnets, which were joined to each other in rough drafts of uncertain date, resemble the five sonnets printed by Meynell as *Ad Amicam,* as well as the sonnets printed by Connolly in the "poetic sequence" and in the miscellaneous sonnet section. One of these, "Love's Varlets," was published by Meynell in the section entitled "Sonnets" that contained the five poems called *Ad Amicam,* but was not joined to that group by him. The companion piece, "Love, Thou Hast Suffered," was printed by Connolly, who identified its association with "Love's Varlets."

Still other works that have been published independently as whole poems would seem actually to be parts of incomplete sonnets. One, appearing in Connolly's section called "A Miscellany" as a ten-line poem "Joy of Life and Death," is, as Walsh observed, part of a sonnent, one quatrain of which appears on the previous page of the notebook in which the penciled draft exists.[25]

In a letter to Meynell written in the fall of 1900 Thompson defended the artistic merit of his poems to Katie. Meynell had apparently criticized them adversely—perhaps not so much because he disliked them as because Mrs. King wanted their publication to be discouraged.[26] Thompson suggested that the poems be viewed collectively, as comparable to his earlier sequences. Moreover, he proposed that Meynell had misjudged them because he viewed them from the wrong perspective. They were not to be seen as a "second edition" of his poems to Alice Meynell. Uttered from the heart and less consciously artificial, they resembled *A Narrow Vessel* more than *Love in Dian's Lap,* being "a kind of poetic diary; or rather a poetic substitute for letters." Because of their directness and familiarity Thompson likened them to Shakespeare's sonnet sequence rather than to Dante's more formally arranged and allegorical *Vita Nuova.* Not "attempted eulogies" of Katie, they were instead "little safety-valves through which my momentary self escaped." While judging their style "much lower, and more casual and subjective" than that of the elaborate *Love in Dian's Lap,* Thompson recognized the intimacy and naturalness that ensure their success.[27]

Although in his 1889 essay "The Way of Imperfection" Thompson had disparaged the fondness among late nineteenth-century poets for fixed forms, including the sonnet, which emphasized polish rather than innovation and imaginative intensity, he had begun experimenting with sonnets very early. A series of four poems collected under the title "On the Anniversary of Rossetti's Death," probably written in 1883 or 1884 and copied into the Notebook of Early Poems, praises Rossetti's contribution to English literature and art of such "Southern" qualities as color and a fiery heart. Thompson commemorates Rossetti the sonneteer in interesting variations on the Italian sonnet form, using iambic tetrameter lines arranged in an untraditionally rhymed octave and sestet.[28] In another early sonnet inspired by Rossetti's canvas *Ecce Ancilla Domini*, which was acquired by the National Gallery in 1886, Thompson reveals a talent, important to many later poems, for treating religious themes by means of pictorial detail rather than statements of doctrine (*MHW*, 39).

The sonnet "Sad Semele," published first in 1957, may well have been written soon after Thompson left his friend the prostitute to begin his career as a poet. Like the best of his sonnets it focuses on a single metaphor, in this instance the union beween Zeus and his mortal paramour Semele. Thompson uses the myth to describe the uneven matching of two lovers. Like Semele, who delivered Zeus's child, the lady of the sonnet inspired the speaker's progeny, poetry. But also like Semele, she was destroyed by their union because she lacked adequate perception to appreciate the poetic accomplishment to which he had contributed.[29]

Another early work, *"Non Pax—Expectatio"* (*Poems*, 2:184), published in the July 1889 *Merry England*, depicts life's uncertainty in arresting imagery. The speaker feels that peace is but "the gap between two lightnings," when "the pulses sicken" and "Thy heart's tomb yawns and renders up its dead,— / The hopes 'gainst hope embalmèd in its womb." When Thompson was enduring drug withdrawal and making his first concentrated efforts as a publishing poet at Storrington, he expressed his sense of isolation in the unpublished *"Cor Meum,"* its fourteen lines of iambic pentameter couplets being a variant of the sonnet form.[30] The poem contrasts the capacity of the speaker's heart with the world's mistaken assessment of its narrowness. These promising early sonnets and variations on standard patterns anticipate some fine sonnets among the love poems addressed to Katie King.

The five sonnets published by Meynell as *Ad Amicam* (*Poems,* 2:171–75) establish the character of what might have been intended as a larger sonnet sequence. The first, admirably unified, metaphorically describes the beloved as a dove who, returning to the speaker's ark, brings peace and hope. Yet the lover anticipates the pain that he must feel if his "heart should hear no white wings thrill / Against its waiting window, open still!" The allusion to Noah's flood, the divine chastisement of human wickedness, provides a moving context for the speaker's nicely understated recollections of his own past folly, and for his view of the woman as an emissary of salvation.

The second *Ad Amicam* sonnet develops a metaphor used in the much earlier lyric "Song of the Hours." Depicting dreams as bees which carry honey "from the blossoms of the noiseful day / Unto the hive of sleep," the speaker declares that the "wildest honey" is "stolen" from the "strange sweet of ever-blossomy you." This tribute to the lady emphasizes her role as his "friend," an appellation developed in the third *Ad Amicam* sonnet. The lover stresses the continuing importance of the woman's friendship, even though "so swift on friend and friend broke love." Throughout the lyrics and sonnets addressed to Katie King, the term *friend* figures more prominently and meaningfully than *lover.* Continuing the theme, the fourth sonnet similarly boasts that this verse will declare to "after-livers . . . / How friends could love for immortality." The sonnets depict love as "a sudden ambush" which in some sense threatens the even more valuable friendship of the lovers.

The fifth sonnet of *Ad Amicam,* in the manuscript entitled "Of My Friend's Aura," extols the lady's heavenly scent, perhaps literally a perfume. Although some of the imagery echoes other sonnets in the series, the hyperbolic language and rather trivial point of this poem highlight the superiority of the first four sonnets.

The four poems grouped by Connolly as "A Poetic Sequence" (*MHW,* 19–21) continue the themes and patterns of *Ad Amicam.* "Elijah," the first of these sonnets, echoes the first sonnet of *Ad Amicam* by developing a biblical analogy and the image of the woman as a ministering bird. The lover, like the prophet Elijah to whom "God sent the bird far-visitant which fed / His bitter need," has been inspirited by his friend's "gentlest succour." "Waiting," the one lyric in the Connolly grouping that is not a sonnet, describes the lover's fears as he awaits the woman's return. In his loneliness his thoughts are frozen, "as weeds in waters are / Congealed with severe frost."

Without the consoling thaw brought by the lady, whom he associates with sun and summer skies, the lover recognizes the mocking contrast between her warmth and his own "palpable chill."
The sonnet "Foregoing" continues the theme of the speaker's isolation from his friend, echoing the flight imagery of both "Elijah" and the *Ad Amicam* sonnets. Beginning "The white wings come no more," it articulates his reaction to the lady's rejecting him. His forlorn resignation becomes especially poignant in light of his gratitude that she cheered him temporarily, as when "A butterfly, that brushes some dark thing, / Some dusty splendour leaves unto its keeping." In "Foregoing" Thompson successfully varies the Shakespearean sonnet form, which he uses in most of the sonnets of this period. Here he concentrates the touching effect of the butterfly image by repeating a single rhyme throughout the third quatrain.

The evidence of thematic and metaphoric kinships between a substantial number of love sonnets suggests the possibility that at some point Thompson intended to form the miscellaneous lyrics written out of his love for Katie King into a sonnet sequence. Moreover, his early experimentation with traditional sonnet forms suggests the possibility of including several manuscript poems of uncertain date in the proposed sonnet sequence.

Perhaps the most interesting is a poem entitled *"Valete"* (*MHW*, 29):

> We have been comrades, and I dwelled with you;
> You have been sportful, and I played with you;
> You have been mirthful, and I laughed with you;
> You have been tearful, and I kissed with you;
> You have been selfful, and I bare with you;
> You have been loveful, and I loved with you;
> You have been strifeful, and I strove with you:
> Now it is ended, and I part with you.
> You have been happy, you and I with you,
> And many happy flowers bear home with you;
> I my one flower, and my one flower is dead.

In eleven lines it may be seen as a resourceful and dramatically effective abbreviation of the sonnet form using the same rhyme word in the first ten lines. After the opening word *we*, suggesting a union between the lovers, the first eight lines define that *we* as the separate elements *you* and *I*. The prominence of *you* at the beginning of seven

lines and at the end of all lines but the last, reveals the speaker's sense
that the lady has dominated the relationship. *We* has remained the
separate *you* and *I* because of her egocentrism and caprice. The phrase
"you and I" in line 9 echoes the kernel structure of lines 2 through
7, with the woman's dominance again emphasized, and the resulting
condition of the relationship abruptly defined as *dead*. The speaker
cannot continue beyond this finality to complete the expected fourteen lines.

Other brief pieces edited from manuscripts may likewise be seen as
fragments of sonnets. "This Vessel Man" (*MHW*, 25), for example,
may be a quatrain and concluding couplet of a sonnet that metaphorically compares a man who has lost his love to a vessel whose precious
cargo has been removed, leaving it listing dangerously. Another
verse, "As Morning Eyes from Sleep Awakening" (*MHW*, 28), eight
lines of blank verse with a ninth line of iambic trimeter, may well be
complete. Yet it may also represent an unfinished experiment in a
blank verse sonnet. Closely echoing the imagery concluding the first
Ad Amicam sonnet, it compares the lover's bleak view of a future
without the woman to the desolation of a window once irradiated by
sunlight but now "Closing again to darkness." In itself, the echo of
the first *Ad Amicam* sonnet does not necessarily link these nine lines
to the sequence, for Thompson frequently revived images he had used
in earlier work, as when the second sonnet of Meynell's *Ad Amicam*
sequence echoes the bee/dream imagery of "Song of the Hours," or
when other lyrics employ imagery also found in his prose. The reference to "the brief irradiant four year's glimpse" of love helps date the
poem, however, for Thompson courted Katie King from 1896 to
1900.

The regular Shakespearean sonnet that concludes Connolly's edition
of "A Poetic Sequence" deepens the pathos of the preceding sonnet,
"Foregoing." In "So Now, Give O'er" the rejected lover grieves that
his offspring Joy was stillborn. Yet this dramatic conclusion does not
end the outpourings that constituted Thompson's "poetic diary" or
"safety-valves" during the ill-fated romance with Katie King.

"A Bitter Friend" (*MHW*, 39), found in the *Ad Amicam* notebook,
continues the theme in the *Ad Amicam* poems that the lovers' friendship was independent of their amorous attraction. The speaker ostensibly apologizes for the "rash" speech and "unfixed" mood in which
he confesses his passion, wounding her tender feelings as the "gray-
green Holly of the Sea" with its harsh rind wounds "tender touches."

The couplet concludes that since he cannot be severed from his loving heart, or be "repured," she had better part with him. Three remaining sonnets in the Connolly collection extend the theme that the lover has transgressed by confessing his love. All specifically associate the frank avowals that offend his beloved with his poetic utterances. "Alack! My Deep Offence" (*MHW*, 40), also in the *Ad Amicam* notebook, uses a military metaphor to suggest that his capitulation to the words that offend the lady paradoxically constitutes his poetic victory. He grieves that his "within-turmoil" inflicts pain on her, but also recognizes that "deep offence is kneaded in / Even with the very stuff of poetry."

Although the next two sonnets exist only in penciled rough drafts and were not copied into the *Ad Amicam* notebook, their affinities with the sonnets gathered there suggest some kinship. "What Have I Left" (*MHW*, 40–41) associates itself with Katie King by referring to the earlier sequences that had been addressed to another woman. The poet recognizes that the woman he now addresses might question the sincerity of these poems because in the past he spoke similarly to someone else. He turns a pretty compliment by suggesting that because the woman he now addresses surpasses even so fine a person as her predecessor, whose virtues he had honestly praised, his exhausted verbal riches can scarcely do her justice: "thine estimate, / Friend, I can match not from my bankrupt store / Who Song's mere prodigal before thee stand, / His gold all spent and no price in his hand." Measured against the studied elaborateness of *Love in Dian's Lap*, this comparative understatement demonstrates the success of Thompson's verbal and metaphoric economy throughout the later love poems. "My Song's Young Virgin Date" (*MHW*, 41) echoes the theme of "What Have I Left." The lady celebrated in his earlier verse provides him a measure by which to gauge the excellence of his present friend.

A number of other works published in Connolly's collection explore topics clearly related to those of the *Ad Amicam* notebook. "Love, Thou Hast Suffered" (*MHW*, 42–43), for example, published from a rough pencil draft, may well belong to the sequence. Like most of the others a regular Shakespearean sonnet, it picks up the bird imagery of *Ad Amicam* and extends the comparison between the present love and the lover's previous relationship with another woman. If the poem has specific biographical reference, as most seem to have, Thompson may be contrasting Katie King with Maggie Brien, for as in *A Narrow Vessel* his principal topic is a lover's insincerity. Although the earlier

object of his affections committed "the sacrilegion of a dallying kiss,"
he—whatever other wrongs he may have done the lady of this sonnet—has never "held [her] light," nor has he ever betrayed her,
though the previous lady betrayed him. This poem was written to
precede "Love's Varlets," which was published among the miscellaneous sonnets in Meynell's 1913 collection (*Poems*, 2:183). "Love's
Varlets" echoes the theme of "A Bitter Friend" and "Alack! My Deep
Offence," for the lover insists that although he has transgressed the
moralist's "rule and line" by speaking of his feelings against the
woman's wishes, he is "nearer" her heart than another man who,
"chill-wrapt / In thy light-thought-on customed livery, / Keeps all
thy laws with formal service apt"—except for the law of loving.

It seems likely that poems scattered in the posthumously published
editions of Meynell and Connolly and in the as yet unprinted manuscripts constitute a fairly ambitious series of sonnets. Like the example of Shakespeare's sonnets invoked by Thompson, and like Rossetti's
sequence, which may also have influenced them, these sonnets do not
record a chronological story. Instead, they register varied emotions in
differing tones, but achieve unity through recurring themes and metaphoric patterns. Thompson's sonnets also reveal interesting experimentation with sonnet conventions. Most significant, they abandon
the courtly conventions and elevated language that originally defined
the sonnet sequence and made Thompson's earliest lyric sequence,
Love in Dian's Lap, artistically interesting but emotionally distant.
While hardly rivaling Shakespeare's accomplishment, Thompson's
sonnets are always competent, often technically interesting, and
sometimes extremely poignant. If he had polished them for publication, they would doubtless have shone even more impressively.

Completely demoralized after Katie's marriage to another man,
Thompson in the summer of 1900 planned to return to the streets
and give himself up to the drug addiction into which he had relapsed.
He wrote Meynell a maudlin and hyperbolic letter evaluating the sonnets to Katie King: "I do think they are rather, *rather* beautiful. I
may be quite wrong, but it does seem to me that they are
good. . . . If I am right it is a crime they cannot be published." And
later, the "*terrible* step I am about to take . . . is lightened with an
inundating joy by the new-found hope that here, in these poems, is
treasure—or at least some measure of beauty that I did not know
of."[31] Thompson mentioned that Katie had once approved their being
printed. But within a year Katie had died, and Thompson lacked the

sense of purpose to renew plans for publishing another volume of poetry. The "treasure" he saw in the love poems has not yet been fully mined.

The Poet of Children, Nature, and God

Describing the projected *First Fruits and Aftermath,* Thompson specified that the collection (if "published during my life and under my supervision") would feature in "a special section towards the end" all his poems to children. He had chosen a motto from Shelley's poem "The Cloud" and written a poem to explain the title of the section, "In the Gardens of Phosphorus." Termed "a dedicatory poem to children in general," *"Stellis Matutinis Humanis"* develops the conceit that children are like "Stars of the Morning" fallen from heaven, God's "Covenant of forgiving love." As in many of the previously collected poems on children, Thompson contrasts their innocence with his fallen state, a "spirit toiled / In a body spent and foiled."[32]

One of the later poems to children, perhaps written in September 1900 but published in the August 1901 *Monthly Review,* is a sequel to the early work "The Poppy," which had similarly described the adult. "To Monica: After Nine Years" (*Poems,* 2:212) contrasts the girl of the present with the former child "full of willy-nillies, / Pets, and bee-like angers: / Flaming like a dusky poppy, / In a wrathful bloom." Several of the poems never collected by Thompson emphasize these erratic mood shifts of the child, the sour curd which balances the strawberry's natural sweetness. In "Love and the Child" (*Poems,* 1:175), first published in the New York *Catholic World* in June 1896, a peevish child who resists caresses reminds the speaker of his own resistance to God, echoing a motif in "The Hound of Heaven." "An Unamiable Child" (*MHW,* 34) focuses on "A child unsweet of face or air" whose unlovable character elicits the poet's love. Again his experience with the child reveals the condition of the speaker, for if he were to lose this "nothing," he would lose all.

The posthumously published "*De Mortuis*" (*MHW,* 32) lightly treats the aging process memorialized in "To Monica: After Nine Years." Only recently a child, the girl of the poem today seems older than the sea "Which scurfed the dragon-pressed seaweed." The speaker mocks the girl's confidence that she knows a great deal: "you can lesson the white head to-day! / And sedulous Science shall expound." But this irony ultimately turns on itself, for the speaker rec-

ognizes that her innocence is somehow more profoundly wise than the
learning of her elders, who "root" for knowledge although death, the
"great master," will teach them soon enough. The ostensible jest that
the girl has grown so suddenly that she now towers over the mountain from which Noah saw "A drowned world's face up-float" suggests
the superior vantage point afforded by her superior moral stature.

A theme introduced in the simple lyric "To Olivia" (*Poems,* 1:20),
that innocence or vulnerability exerts a frightening power, acquires
dimension in "To Daisies" (*Poems,* 2:191), first published in the *English Review* and the *Atlantic Monthly* in July 1910. Though not so
clearly focused as these other poems on childhood, this lyric evokes
the adult's nostalgia for his own lost innocence, represented by the
daisy. But the blossom also becomes the catalyst for others' figurative
loss of innocence, for children tantalized by its beauty pluck its pet-
als. Thompson underscores the sexual suggestions of the image by
specifically comparing the daisy to "Weak maids, with flutter of a
dress," who "do not know [their] power for wrong" and exercise
"most heavy tyrannies." The poem may be read as an indirect expression of the adult's sexual guilt. Like many of Thompson's works, "To
Daisies" associates childhood with Nature, another of his frequent
topics.

"To Stars" (*Poems,* 1:198), which similarly combines Nature and
childhood, is more complex and more skillful. Like most of the
poems to children published in Thompson's 1893 volume, "To Stars"
arose from a specific incident, the serious injury sustained by young
Viola Meynell when she fell over a banister to a floor below. The
poet's musing on the hurt child's inability to respond to his gift of
flowers evokes the theme of an individual's inability to appreciate a
love "too high" for full comprehension. This theme, familiar
throughout Thompson's poetry, receives particularly fresh and interesting treatment here. The poem begins with imagery of the cosmic
scale found in much of his early verse. The speaker contemplates the
stars, which the injured child cannot see, as signs by which God reveals himself to blind men, "Bright juts for foothold to the climbing
sight." As his thoughts focus on the child, however, the tone and
imagery modulate to the gentle, small, and familiar. Represented in
the pathetic figure of the unresponsive child, man's "Oedipean"
blindness to the message of the stars is shown to be not willful resistance but vulnerability.

Like the stars in this poem, Nature in other works reveals God. Thompson presents this message directly in a simple poem like "I Sat with Nature" (*MHW*, 51), where the uncertain tone of the last line lends interest to the speaker's recognition that Nature speaks not for man's pleasure but for God. In "Sing, Bird, Sing" Thompson the lyricist joins with Nature to praise God in serenade (*MHW*, 54).

Unlike these simple lyrics, the ode "Of Nature: Laud and Plaint" (*Poems*, 2:162) uses the complex, elevated language characteristic of the odes in Thompson's collections. Investigating the relationship of Nature to man and God, it specifically challenges the view of Nature posited by Romantic poets—especially Wordsworth, whose works it echoes. Describing Nature as "God's daughter," who "lends / Her hand but to His friends" (phrasing used also in his prose "Nature's Immortality"), Thompson insists that "she nor gives nor teaches; / She suffers thee to take / But what thine own hand reaches." As he divests Nature of any claim to divinity in her own right, Thompson emphasizes the reality of the God whom Nature manifests.

In contrast to this ambitious but uninspired ode, "All Flesh" (*Poems*, 2: 224) demonstrates how effectively Thompson, using simple language, could invest a single image with large meanings. The speaker's "foundering mind" discovers an "Odyssean fate" in contemplating a single blade of grass. The mythological allusion implies that scrutiny of this commonplace emblem opens for him a world of epic proportion, and also that this voyage of discovery brings him safely home from turbulent experiences. Enumerating the aspects of Nature that have nurtured the grass-blade, the speaker implies the harmony of the universe, as well as the importance of all that appears insignificant: "And such a god of grass! / A little root clay-caught, / A wind, a flame, a thought, / Inestimably naught!"

Although the implications of Thompson's blade of grass in some ways echo the meanings of Walt Whitman, the contrasts between Whitman's point and poetics and Thompson's are compactly illustrated by Thompson's metaphoric explanation of his central symbol: "Epitomized in thee / Was the mystery / Which shakes the spheres conjoint— / God focussed to a point."[33]

The poems that concentrate more directly on God's nature demonstrate Thompson's tonal variety. In "A Faithless Sword" (*MHW*, 57) the speaker compares himself to a weapon that has failed his God, who is stirringly described as a warrior. A similarly militant image appears in a late poem "The Veteran of Heaven," printed with *"Lilium Regis"* in the January 1910 *Dublin Review* under the collective title "Ecclesiastical Ballads" (*Poems,* 1:149–51). "The Veteran of Heaven" develops the paradox familiar in medieval tradition that through the Crucifixion "the Slain hath the gain, and the Victor hath the rout." The companion poem proclaims the impious present a period of the Virgin's "unqueening" and prophesies upheaval and bloodshed: "Lo, the hour is at hand for the troubling of the land, / And red shall be the breaking of the waters . . . / When the nations lie in blood, and their kings a broken brood." Although readers have interpreted these lines as prediction of the impending world war—and Thompson's prose records his awareness of troubling political situations in Europe—the rhetoric recalls Old Testament condemnations of impious nations.

In contrast to the militant God of these lyrics, God the humane caretaker figures in "He Came to Me," "Madonna and Child," and "Weep for Him" (*MHW,* 58–60), all of which evoke the comforting mystery of the Incarnation in terms reminiscent of *"Ex Ore Infantium"* ("Little Jesus"). An extended metaphor in "Weep for Him" suggests the generosity of a ministering God. When man "took, in malice, to his tainted vein, / Sin, and its legacy of lazarous pain," God kissed "the infected flesh" to "suck the venom from the ulcerous place," allowing man "on his sick-bed, earth" to "fever through his pain."

God's immanence in man provides the theme of an effective early sonnet *"Desiderium Indesideratum,"* published in *Merry England* in June 1893 (*Poems,* 2:182). Distraught by the apparent elusiveness of God, the speaker quits searching the "unmarged arcane," only to discover in himself the truth he sought: "I looked. My claspèd arms athwart my breast / Framed the august embraces of the Cross." In this poem Thompson varies the Petrarchan sonnet for a striking effect. By isolating the final word *Cross* with an extremely slant rhyme, he stresses the uniqueness of the Incarnation and Crucifixion as proofs of divine love.

Awareness of human limitation tinges the nicely focused work *"Nisi Dominus"* (*MHW,* 30), which alludes to both a building metaphor in Psalms and the tower of Babel story. Although human beings attempt to build an edifice of communication, "Unless the Holy One its keystone be," the dwelling will fall: "Confusion of tongues is come on us, God wot! / And that which I would speak, thou understandest not."

Such sobriety does not characterize all of Thompson's religious verse. "The Schoolmaster for God" (*MHW*, 69–72), for example, which was printed in part in the April 1913 issue of the *Irish Rosary*, describes Satan's gaining influence over humanity in a lighthearted narrative embellished from the opening stanza with linguistic play: "the devil girned as he lurched his hoof / Over the border-wall, / The border-wall of the guarded garth / That is God's garth withal." The poem affirms that by schooling man in the wages of sin, Satan labors in God's employ.

The Poet on the Poet

Although best known for his fervor, Thompson penned a great deal of light verse. Much of it is pure doggerel, but a number of poems reveal a genuine comic spirit, alternately sophisticated and impish. Especially fond of puns, he humorously satirized topics ranging from an editor who annoyed him ("Cust," *LP*, 78), to inflated language ("Limerick, Refined," *LP*, 79), and the tall tales of travel narratives (" 'The Voice of the Turtle Is Heard in Our Land,' " (*MHW*, 83–84). Even his poetic craft, usually a serious subject, occasionally prompted levity. "The Poet Jester" (*MHW*, 81) considers whether a poet may lay aside his formal robes to don the jester's bells. Although his readers expect earnestness, the poet queries, "Must one *always* work nought else / Than the high phantastic spells?" His usual themes, "Paul and Pauline matter," produce "the kind of clatter / Sends us sheer / Crazy as a cross between a March Hare and a Hatter." In this poem Thompson echoes the medieval tradition that presented the poet as a fool, especially as God's fool. Elsewhere he uses a light touch to defend his more usual serious style. "On a Reviewer, Calling My Poetry 'Ambitious' " (*MHW*, 89–90) rebukes a critic's pompous pronouncement by pointing to Nature for examples of trees and stars and birds that reach high not in conscious effort but simply because they naturally soar: "I never yet to think did pause / Were my song high or low; / And I attempt the sky because / My pinions bear me so."

More seriously, Thompson defended the metaphoric reach of his typical style in a brief poem "A-Fume with Fire" (*LP*, 68). Criticizing sterile poetry in which the "vein-drawn hues" have "lost heart to shine," he prefers richly metaphoric verse in which the "bee a-fume

with fire" burns on the spiced pyre of the rose. Elsewhere he criticizes
the current tendency to reject lofty poetic style and lofty thought.
"No Singer of His Time" (*MHW*, 90–91) seems particularly poignant
in its obvious application to Thompson, who was so often lambasted
for his archaic diction and declared a throwback to the seventeenth
century. In purposely common, contemporary language Thompson
defends the high-principled craftsman. Because the poet in the poem
does not share the aesthetic and spiritual bankruptcy of his contemporaries, they brand him "No singer of his time / Not of to-day, nor
yet of any day." "Nourished upon the husks of threshed-out things,"
he produces only "an ineffectual rhyme": "His muse he will not
tire / Upon the entrails of the unclean ideals / Which serve for us."
Beginning with a stark and stirring charge against ignorant readers,
the poem combines Thompson's social and artistic criticisms:

> Ye have denied
> Ye have denied
> Ye have denied
> Ye have denied
> Nothing at all is of august and high,
> Allaying man's dull dust, ye not deny.

This defense of his unfashionable style takes a strikingly modern
form.

The theme that society misunderstands and undervalues the poet
recurs throughout Thompson's uncollected and unpublished verse.
Three terse allegorical couplets called "I Showed to All My Goodly
Fruit" (*MHW*, 89) maintain that the crowd prefers the husk and rind
of poetry which merely shows "Things as they Are" to the "Fruit of
Paradise" purveyed by the idealist or visionary. "The Water to the
Star Returns" (*MHW*, 93), two quatrains and a concluding couplet
(perhaps a fragment of a sonnet), likens the poet to God in being unappreciated: "the great love is ever least beloved." "Genesis" (*MHW*,
52–54), like "All Flesh," invests a common image with deep significance. Its simple quatrains of tetrameter couplets trace the life of a
little brown seed to create an allegory of the neglected poet. He creates beauty for the world to enjoy but himself remains unprized.

Elsewhere Thompson stresses the limitations of the poet. In
"Deeply-Sinning Man" (*MHW*, 92) the poet recognizes that although

he can perceive the highest ideals, he is humanly corrupt. If people could see beyond his pose, they would shun him like dead carrion. Five heroic couplets entitled "A Fool by Nature and by Art" (*MHW,* 94) mock the poet's effort to "supplement" the meager man with the poet's "small line, with dainty exquisiteness / Of feeble polish, polished feebleness." His art merely magnifies the fool.

"A Poet's Testament" (*MHW,* 95–96) also acknowledges the human weakness of the poet. Leaving behind him "nothing, nothing / . . . But some poor pleasances of word-enclosed / And much-toil-ordered thought," he will like all men bequeath to the earth a body already "entailed / On the prodigal worm." Even while announcing the ephemerality of his body and his poetry, however, the speaker implies that his works have genuine value, though succeeding generations may ignore them "as unregardfully / As those that in their daily multitudes / Pass by, unaware, occulted Paradise."

As often as he complains of being unappreciated, the speaker in Thompson's verse laments lack of inspiration. Several early works, published in *Merry England* but not subsequently reprinted, express this grief, perhaps reflecting Thompson's own periodic sense of faltering powers. In "A Broom-branch at Twilight," published in November 1891, the speaker describes the flower as a recalcitrant keeper of Nature's secrets who refuses to inspire him. But the poet himself proves to be responsible for this creative impasse. As he describes the elements that refuse to inspire him, the poet attributes to them the spiritual frost that prevents him from hearing his own heart's "hid tongue." A year later Thompson again expressed the failure of poetic inspiration that plagued him after the first dazzling rush of poems such as "Ode to the Setting Sun" and "The Hound of Heaven." "How the Singer's Singing Wailed for the Singer," subtitled "A Dream-Transcript" (November 1892, *Merry England*), personifies the poet's song as a lady whom the poet nurtured from childhood to become his bride, but abandoned just when she reached the age for fulfillment in marriage.

"An Allegory (Of Poetic Composition)," never published by Thompson (*LP,* 80–81), similarly personifies poetic song. It describes the poet's wooing art as a man's troubled mating with a woman who in the boudoir coyly resists his overtures. Beneath the ludic surface, however, the poem suggests the sad alienation of the poet. Having sacrificed human love for the sake of his writing, he lies abed "wedded" to his art.

"O Fair and Affluent Sabbath of My Muse" (*MHW*, 94–95) describes this poetic silence in more stately metaphors. The speaker, whose inspiration has dried up, stands like "A fountained nymph, whose lips are still a-stretch / In carven waiting for the wonted stream / Which no more shall her desolated mouth / Wet," become a "wide-lipped figure of memorial drouth." Addressing the Meynells, Thompson chastises himself for having lacked humility when inspiration blessed him freely. The first half of the poem reveals his talent for mixing metaphors to achieve a single impression. His very lack of inspiration often inspired effective verse.

The Poet of Contemporary Events

Even before poetic inspiration actually faltered, however, Thompson seemed to the public to have stopped writing serious poetry. After 1900 and the desolation of losing Katie King, he remained busy with book reviews. Most of the little poetry that appeared in print was either trivial work such as "Dress," a jingly commentary on women's fashions (published in *T. P.'s Weekly*, 27 February 1903, and not reprinted), or occasional verse commissioned by the press.

Even during this apparently fallow period, however, Thompson wrote at least one very fine poem, "The Kingdom of God" (*Poems*, 2:226–27).[34] Finished by late 1903 and perhaps begun as much as a year earlier, this striking poem remained unknown until nine months after Thompson's death, when it appeared in the August 1908 *Athenaeum*. A neatly crafted series of six quatrains attests God's immanence. Rather than asking "the stars in motion / If they have rumour" of God, we must listen to the spirit that "Beats at our own clay-shuttered doors." Jacob's ladder is "Pitched betwixt Heaven and Charing Cross"; Christ walks "on the water / Not of Gennesareth, but Thames." This poem shows the mature poet at his best, still capable of richly evocative imagery and memorable phrasing ("the many-splendoured thing"), yet quietly disciplined.

While "The Kingdom of God" remained unknown, however, the press published a number of adequate but uninspired occasional poems. From early in his poetic career Thompson had written poetry for newsworthy events at the request of Wilfrid Meynell and editors of other journals to which he regularly contributed. Although Thompson disparaged commissioned work because "to write verses to order . . . precludes all chance of its being poetry,"[35] he had in his years of greater creativity penned some good poetry on commission. "To the Dead Cardinal of Westminster" and "A Dead Astronomer," for example, both transcend ordinary obituary verse in thematic significance and verbal achievement. But not all his commemorative verse succeeded so well. His early poem on the death of Cardinal Newman, "John Henry Newman" (*Weekly Register*, 16 August 1890), is a fairly doctrinaire exercise praising the cardinal as a human sacrifice to the rebuilding of the Church in England. Despite his reluctance to write such poetry on order, Thompson was rather proud of having "knocked off three little stanzas" within a few hours of Meynell's request.[36]

He also quickly prepared the 300-line "Ode for the Diamond Jubilee of Queen Victoria" (*Daily Chronicle*, 27 June 1897; *Poems*, 2:137–45). Written "within the space of a few days," the surprisingly competent poem seemed to Thompson an "uninspired imitation of myself."[37] Conceived as a visionary pageant of figures representing the achievements of the era, the poem derives from a classical tradition passed through Petrarch's *Triumphs*. Thompson predictably grows most specific on the subject of literary accomplishments, singling out as the finest poets of the age Tennyson, the Brownings, Arnold, Christina and Dante Gabriel Rossetti, and—in the longest passage—Coventry Patmore. He characterizes Browning and Arnold succinctly but with particularly apt insight.

At least one occasional poem seems to have arisen not from commission but from Thompson's own shock at a contemporary event. "The House of Sorrows" expresses the pathos of the assassination of the Empress of Austria on 10 September 1898. The poem remained unpublished until it appeared in the *Dublin Review* in January 1911, over twelve years after the event and three years after Thompson's death.[38]

To commemorate the turn of the century, Thompson filled a commission from the *Academy*. "Forced . . . under a narrow time-limit," "The Nineteenth Century" (*Poems*, 2:146) nonetheless seemed to Thompson a tour de force.[39] Succinctly cataloguing the great conflicts of the passing century, especially the Darwinian controversy, and concluding with a hope for military peace, the ode stresses scientific advances as the greatest achievements of the century.

"Peace" (*Poems*, 2:153), commissioned by the *Daily Chronicle*, commemorates the signing of the treaty to end the Boer War. Though written in less than a week and set in type four days before the signing of the treaty on 31 May 1902, the poem was never published, perhaps because it subordinates patriotic fervor to an ominous warning that England must guard against the greed that led to war in South Africa. Earlier, in 1898, Thompson had written "To England," commissioned by the *Academy* (published on 19 March; not reprinted), ninety lines that exhort the nation to stand firm against the Boers. In the same month as the Boer treaty was signed, Thompson prepared a poem to commemorate the death of Cecil Rhodes, the empire builder in South Africa. Commissioned on 26 March, the day Rhodes died, and printed on 12 April 1902, "Cecil Rhodes" (*Poems,* 2:157) forthrightly acknowledges the materialism and egotism of its subject but admires his capacity to dream enlarging dreams. The social criticism undergirding "Cecil Rhodes" and "Peace" finds direct and forceful expression in poems published only posthumously such as "England, Old and New," "God! If Thou Sitt'st in Heaven," and *"Fuit"* (*MHW,* 64–65), which especially condemn materialism and urge the nation to live up to its glorious heritage.

Perhaps the last written of Thompson's occasional poems is "Ode to the English Martyrs" (*Poems,* 2:131), commissioned by the *Dublin Review* and published in April 1906. Written painstakingly after Thompson had been sent by Meynell to the Franciscan monastery at Crawley to reduce his laudanum consumption, the poem honors the Catholic martyrs slain in the religious controversies under the Tudor and Stuart monarchs. The ode measures how much Thompson's poetic fire had subsided by the last two years of his life. It begins with the visual image of Tyburn tree, the infamous gallows on which hundreds of Catholics were martyred. His tepid treatment of this emblem contrasts forcefully with the highly charged description of the Storrington crucifix that had ignited his first remarkable poem, "Ode to the Setting Sun."

Thompson's low evaluation of "To the English Martyrs" points up the poignancy of his poetic silence after 1900, for his comments contrast starkly with his hopes, expressed a decade earlier, of publishing another volume of poetry: "Shouldn't dream of publishing it (in book, I mean). If any poetry *has* got into it, it is a pity; I intended best silver-gilt, & *that* is wasteful—brass much cheaper, & preferred for commercial purposes."[40] Even so, he still claimed some poetic power: "the *Dublin* might go further & fare a great deal worse. Even in my ashes, I think there lives a little more fire than in any other Catholic versifier of whom I know." Yet he also acknowledged that writing the poem had exhausted him. He could not revise lines Meynell criticized: "The last reserve of power I could husband was discharged into them."[41]

Thompson's poetic resourcefulness and physical stamina were near to exhaustion. Within six weeks of this letter the last poem to be published in his lifetime appeared in the *Nation* on 6 April 1907. Probably also the last poem he wrote, "The Fair Inconstant" (*Poems*, 1:220) resembles one of the first poems he ever sent to Meynell in that it records the speaker's love longing. Yet, unlike "Dream-Tryst," this lyric does not dream of reunion with an idealized figure. The speaker bluntly contends that he has created the beauty on which his inconstant lady prides herself: "But thou too late, too late shalt find / 'Twas I that made thee fair; / Thy beauties never from thy mind / But from my loving were."

Hardly a distinguished poem when read simply as a bitter lover's taunt, when read symbolically it fittingly reviews Thompson's publishing career as a poet, which began in "The Passion of Mary" with his adoration of the religious embodiment of the beauty and love his poetry would consistently serve. In the final lines of "The Fair Inconstant" the poet recognizes that with his love and imgination he has invested his subjects with a beauty not their own: "And what I was, not what thou art, / Did gazers-on admire. / Go, and too late thou shalt confess / I looked thee into loveliness!" When Thompson died, shortly before his forty-eighth birthday, he left a cache of unpublished loveliness—and powerful starkness—that still awaits full disclosure.

Chapter Five
Prose

In the year his *New Poems* appeared Francis Thompson penned a significant notebook entry:

1897: End of Poet. Beginning of Journalist.
The years of transition completed.[1]

Although he continued to write poetry, the notebook entry fittingly memorialized his overriding preoccupation with prose in the last decade of his life, a commitment probably stimulated initially by his desire to earn a steady income and, with it, serious consideration as a suitor for Katie King.

Thompson had begun publishing prose and poetry at almost the same time. In fact, the Meynells published his first poem "The Passion of Mary" as a means of establishing contact with the author of an essay they were eager to print in *Merry England*. After Thompson wrote Wilfrid Meynell on 14 April 1888 to say he had learned that his verse had been published, the editor drew the timid, shabby poet to his office by paying a debt at the chemist's shop where Thompson had written he could be reached. They met in mid-May; the essay "Paganism Old and New" appeared in June.

This was only the first of a continuing stream of prose which, in light of both Thompson's commitment to poetry and his recurring physical debilities, must be judged prodigious. A Thompson bibliography prepared by Terence Connolly lists nearly 480 titles of reviews and essays published from 1889 to 1907. Impressive as this figure is, it may not represent his total output, for most of his pieces were published anonymously. Of the nearly 350 reviews which he contributed to the *Academy* between 1896 and 1907, fewer than thirty are signed,[2] and all fifty-four of those printed in the *Athenaeum* (the next most frequent outlet for his reviews) are unsigned.

Similar anonymity prevailed with his earliest contributions to periodicals. Of the sixteen pieces identified as Thompson's in *Merry En-*

gland, for example, only two are signed. Only one of the others is anonymous. Three are signed "Francis Phillimore" and three "Francis Tancred," pen names also used by both Alice and Wilfrid Meynell. The remaining seven are signed "Philip Hemans," a pseudonym apparently used only by Thompson.[3] Of the twenty-one pieces he published from 1890 to 1893 in the Meynells' newspaper the *Weekly Register,* only two carried his name.

From 1897, when Thompson recorded the "Beginning of Journalist," to the year of his death, his prose contributions to periodicals numbered in the double figures annually. The decade began with at least twenty-eight reviews in the first year. In Thompson's final years renewed drug dependency and related ill health dropped the number dramatically, from more than thirty pieces in 1905 to nineteen the following year, and finally to only ten in 1907.

His years of highest productivity in prose extend from 1898, with over forty titles, through 1904, again with over forty. His annual total peaked impressively at more than sixty pieces in both 1901 and 1902, with at least fifty-nine in 1903. During this thirty-six-month period, Thompson usually contributed from four to six reviews per month, a figure which rose in at least five months to eight, and once to nine.

Most of the pieces written in these highly productive years were brief book reviews, but they testify to a heavy load of close reading. In addition, he also attempted at least four plays, one as early as 1891 and two submitted for the Meynells' criticism in 1907. From 1905 a biography of St. Ignatius Loyola, founder of the Jesuit order, occupied Thompson, who had also written an earlier biography called *The Life and Labours of St. John Baptist de la Salle* (published in *Merry England* in 1891). Based largely on encyclopedia articles and biographies in the British Museum, these lives of the saints have been termed "hack-work, being commissions obtained for him by Wilfrid Meynell and conscientiously carried out, under what spurs we do not know, with little real enthusiasm for the subjects."[4]

The biography of Ignatius Loyola, Thompson's longest prose work, was published posthumously in 1909 after having been edited by J. H. Pollen. Writing it when his addiction had reasserted itself, Thompson depended on financial need to regulate his work habits. Wilfrid Meynell instructed his son Everard to pay the poet one pound each time he delivered three pages of completed text.[5]

Thompson's contributions to *Merry England* demonstrate his facility for turning out slight but intelligent articles on assignment. His two pieces in the April 1893 issue, for example, (one signed "Philip Hemans" and the other "Francis Phillimore") illustrate his versatility: "Eve in the Garden" begins by paying tribute to a woman who had recently received an award for her accomplishments in astronomy (she is one of the "gardeners of the stars," an image Thompson would later use in the poem "A Dead Astronomer"), and it ends by discussing Milton's portrait of Eve; "Romans at Table" describes Roman dining customs and daily routine. In addition to such minor journalistic pieces, Thompson wrote a number of essays, most of them early in his career, that deal with literary theory, social criticism, religion, and philosophy. Some of these are extremely interesting, both for their illumination of his poetic themes and artistry and for their literary merit.

In a late book review (1903) Thompson described the essay as "the least formal, the most friendly, personal, and artlessly artistic mode of communication between writer and reader"—"the last word of art's endeavour to join hands with the multitude, before art degenerated into the article" aimed at a select audience.[6] Many of his prose works show the easy familiarity that he characterized as "the arm-chair attitude which is the leading trait of the essay as it was born with Montaigne." His judgment that by his day the essay had "forgotten how to idle wisely, cultivatedly, or wittily" does not describe his own works.[7] They are witty and urbane, and while appearing to ramble in leisurely fashion, they actually lead toward wise and cultivated ends. His essays range widely in subject matter and style, sometimes ascending from the discursive familiarity he enjoyed in Charles Lamb's works to a majestic rhetoric reminiscent of biblical prose.

Christian Paganism

His first published essay, "Paganism Old and New" (June 1888) struggled into print against adversity. Sporadically written on scraps of paper during his time at John McMaster's bootshop and after his return to the streets, it arrived in Meynell's office in a sadly soiled state, hand-carried by Thompson to the mail slot because, he later remembered, when he got down to his last piece of paper, he had only the sum for return postage. The note that accompanied the manuscript reveals his limited expectations: "I enclose a stamped en-

velope for a reply; since I do not desire the return of the manuscript,
regarding your judgment of its worthlessness as quite final."[8] The
manuscript lay neglected for several months before "Paganism Old
and New" arrested the busy editor's attention.[9] The essay attributes
the glory of Western literature to the influence of Christianity, succinctly declaring that "Pagan Paganism was not poetical."[10] One of
Thompson's principal objectives was to defend the poetry of the Romantic unbelievers whom he loved from charges of atheism and paganism.[11] The essay explores the qualities that distinguish
Renaissance and Romantic myth-making from classical treatment of
the same material. His intriguing hypothesis is expressed in forceful,
striking figures that are emotionally if not rationally persuasive.

Although Thompson describes as "pagan" most literature of the
pre-Christian era, the term as he uses it does not really apply to Platonic works, for Platonism in its awareness of a permanent and transcendent Ideal fosters the reverence and love Thompson defines as the
essence of Christianity. Conversely, in the modern era dating from
the advent of Christianity, he characterizes as essentially Christian
works by even avowed non-Christians because the age has imbued
them with an emotional and psychological texture absent from the
practical and earth-centered philosophy of the ancients. Of Shelley he
writes, "the blood in the veins of his Muse was Christian" (*Poems*,
3:47n). Throughout the essay Thompson draws heavily on Platonic
thought, especially as it was filtered through the Romantics.

Perhaps developing an idea suggested by De Quincey's "Modern
Superstition," Thompson argues that beauty was infused into pagan
myth in the Renaissance and in the Romantic period. Pagan literature
was unpoetical because it was not sufficiently beautiful, and it was
not sufficiently beautiful because writers did not love the mythological beings they wrote about. The pagans of antiquity could not love
their gods, Thompson maintains, for although these deities were
"graceful, handsome, noble" and "powerful," they were also "cold in
their sublime selfishness, and therefore unlovable. No Pagan ever
loved his god" (*Poems*, 3:40). Because modern poets in contrast can
love the humanly accessible Madonna and Christ, they can sing true
beauty. In this argument Thompson adapts the Platonic relationship
between Love and Beauty, which holds that the highest form of Love
is devotion to Ideal Beauty, and that love of this Ideal produces beautiful offspring in the mortal world in the form of art, architecture,
poetry, and music.

The devotional attitude of post-pagan poets allows them to treat even pagan material with similarly creative affection: "To the average Pagan, Venus was simply the personification of the generative principle in nature; and her offspring was Cupid,—Desire, Eros—sexual passion." But to "the modern," Venus "is the Principle of Earthly Beauty" (*Poems*, 3:42). Romantic paganism evinces and fosters a love of beauty much as specifically Christian literature does. Thompson's observation of interrelationships between literature and philosophical or religious perspectives leads him to topics such as modern man's superior appreciation of Nature and of female beauty and sexual love. These apparent digressions actually define Thompson's subject as not merely literary uses of classical mythology, but the cultivation of an aesthetic response to life that reflects a cultivated spirituality.[12]

His comments on female beauty and on marriage as an expression of salvation extended by God to man, like his observations on Nature and on the poet's use of pagan mythology, argue specifically against godlessness and licentiousness in art.[13] He also warns against a threatened decline in social morality and artistic beauty, which for him go hand in hand, in contemporary letters. This debasement already afflicts the French: Paganism "already stoops on Paris, and wheels in shadowy menace over England. Bring back *this*—and make of poetry a dancing-girl, and of art a pandar" (*Poems*, 3:50). This condemnation indicates that even as Thompson praises the superiority of modern letters and modern spirituality to those of classical antiquity, he recognizes weaknesses in his own age.

Early in the essay, for example, Thompson distinguishes a sensuous delight in beauty that flourished in pagan antiquity from the comparative aesthetic impoverishment of Victorian society, an impoverishment with religious and social dimensions: "the condition of to-day" involves "cold formalities of an outworn worship," a populace which views "a Lord Mayor's Show" as the "*ne plus ultra* of pageantry" and "dryadless woods . . . as potential timber." Modern society accepts "the grimy street, the grimy air, the disfiguring statues, the Stygian crowd." A figure drawn from pagan myth but laden with the emotional and spiritual value Thompson finds only in Christian, and therefore poetical, paganism summarizes the state of modern industrial society: "Aurora may rise over our cities, but she has forgotten how to blush" (*Poems*, 3:39).

Ironically, when Thompson attempted in his own poetry to combine the aesthetic richness of antiquity with the spiritual substance of Christianity, he was charged with pagan tendencies by exactly the sort of Catholic Philistine to whom he objected in this essay. A canon of the Catholic church printed an attack on Thompson's "Ode to the Setting Sun," a notice soon followed by an anonymous letter warning Wilfrid Meynell against publishing any further work by Francis Thompson, for "it would be found in the end that paganism was at the bottom of it." Thompson archly observed, "This with regard to me, who began my literary career with an elaborate indictment of the ruin which the re-introduction of the pagan spirit must bring upon poetry!"[14]

Even though Thompson asserted the superiority of a Christian moral-aesthetic philosophy to that of classical antiquity, in a 1902 book review he criticized the theory that study of English literature should replace education in the classics. The value of studying classical literature lay not in the works' philosophy or literary merit, however, but in the mental discipline required by translation: "The classics were never a means of teaching boys to love letters; they were a discipline for certain mental faculties, and an unconscious training in the flexible use of language."[15] Moreover, appreciation of poetry, related as it is to an encompassing moral and spiritual health, cannot in fact be taught: "Poetry cannot be taught; but a love for poetry can be germinated, in those who already possess the seed—and in them only" (*RRLS*, 279).

In "Paganism Old and New" Thompson anticipated many of the themes and stylistic techniques that would characterize his poetry and subsequent prose. He maintained that the one valid poetic objective is to create beauty, which in turn necessarily leads readers to recognize higher truths and to love. He suggested that writers can adapt classical materials to Christian ends, and also asserted that whatever the poet's acknowledged philosophical alignment, true poetry is a priori thoroughly consistent with Christian values. His essay thus justifies the combination of Christian and classical elements in his own poetry that his critics sometimes attacked. In addition to establishing this context for his poetry, "Paganism Old and New" also anticipated much of his further prose in its discursive method of integrating topics such as society, Nature, love, poetry, philosophy, and religion.

Decadence and Health

Thompson reiterated the full range of ideas discussed in "Paganism Old and New" in a prose narrative probably begun in the late summer of 1889 and published in the June 1890 issue of *Merry England*.[16]

Unique among his prose as the only tale, *"Finis Coronat Opus"* calls to mind the dark stories of Edgar Allan Poe with its heavy symbolism, its allegory, its supernatural elements, and its grim irony.[17] It relates the history of the poet Florentian, who enacts the fearful possibilities Thompson anticipates at the end of "Paganism Old and New" when renewed paganism threatens to overshadow the Christian texture of modern letters and mores. Dwelling "in a city of the future, among a people bearing a name I know not," Florentian succumbs to the allure of pagan poetry, with the attendant inability to love God, Nature, or woman that Thompson had outlined in the earlier essay. A Faust figure, Florentian has followed "the seductions of knowledge and intellectual pride" and "passed from the pursuit of natural to the pursuit of unlawful science."[18]

Symbols in his private chamber illustrate the conflict between Christian and pagan principles. Florentian eventually desecrates an altar surmounted with the crucifix because he feels stronger devotion to three statues of pagan poets. Significantly, the figure of Virgil—larger than those of Homer and Aeschylus—represents not simply the classical epic poet, but Virgil the magician as he was understood by medieval legend. As the narrator observes, this poet-magus is "the carved embodiment of Florentian's fanatical ambition, a perpetual memento of the double end at which his life was aimed" (*Poems* 3:119). The sculpture depicts Virgil poised as though he is handing both the magician's rod and the poet's crown to a successor.

Though obsessed by desire to win the poet's crown awarded annually by "universal acclaim," Florentian always loses the honor to his principal rival, Seraphin. The symbolic names imply Thompson's allegorical intention: Florentian's name suggests the flowering artistic talents that he hopes will mature into the laurel of fame; Seraphin, described as "a spirit of higher reach than Florentian" (*Poems* 3:116), bears the name of the angels in the Christian hierarchy distinguished by their wisdom. In order to surpass Seraphin in the poetic competition, Florentian seals a Faustian bargain with evil, described as an ominous shadow which "eclipses" the Christian altar, that he will sacrifice the body of his bride. Florentian thus sacrifices love to poetic aspiration, but in symbolic terms he subordinates wisdom and spiritual insight of the sort Thompson would later describe in the *Sight and Insight* section of his 1897 volume, settling instead for popularity. His bargain has more somber philosophical and religious ramifications, however. His bride is named Aster, a symbolic star, and is the child of Urania, a muse of wisdom and poetry whom Thompson would also depict in the 1897 volume. In addition, Urania in classical literature is the muse of astronomy, representing the study of Nature forsaken by Florentian for suspect magic. In a dramatic gesture Florentian gives up his aspirations to the wisdom, science, and true poetry represented by these figures by renouncing Christianity. He violates the crucifix and replaces it with a sculpture resembling Pan derisively sticking out his tongue. Emphasizing the egotism of his renunciation of Christianity, Florentian makes himself a parody of the crucified Christ. He deliberately wounds himself and then consecrates his grimacing new idol by rubbing his own blood on Pan's tongue. The disembodied voice of evil refers to his baptizing himself in his own blood.

When after three years Florentian is about to receive the poet's laurel for which he killed his wife, he falls into a terror of remorse, but—like Marlowe's Faustus—at the eleventh hour he refuses to repent. He meets a fitting end, the details of which highlight the macabre significance of the title, "the thing done is crowned by its end." He finally achieves the only poetic crown for which he is suited when the symbol proffered by the gigantic sculpture of Virgil falls and crushes him.

The prevailingly adverse criticisms of this tale usually characterize it as a symbolic autobiography of Thompson the Decadent.[19] Although its atmosphere and style call to mind such writers as De Quincey, Poe, and Oscar Wilde, and some details clearly draw on Thompson's personal experience, the work criticizes the artistic and philosophical decadence castigated at the end of "Paganism Old and New," in reference to the corrupting influence of the Parisian avant-garde.[20] Thompson elsewhere criticized Aestheticism and Decadence more directly. In a later, unpublished review of a collection of Ernest Dowson's poetry (1905) he mentions the "painful story" of Dowson's life: the "worst follies associated with the literary cafés of Montmartre; from the *haschisch* of Baudelaire to the alcoholism of Verlaine," "prematurely broke to pieces a fragile body and more fragile genius."[21] Although Thompson could lament such personal misfortunes, he quarreled with the literary practices of the Aesthetes and Decadents, exercising a critical judgment quite independent of his sympathies or antipathies for the writers themselves. Reviewing work by Sir Alfred Douglas, for example, he appreciated its beauty, but judged it inferior to "song which has . . . conscious significance." Such evalua-

tions only appear to conflict with his contention in "Paganism Old
and New" that the sole objective of true poetry is beauty, for while
admitting the attractive verbal effects of Douglas's verse, he insisted
that true poetry must contain philosophically beautiful substance.[22]
A brief early work published in the October 1892 issue of *Merry
England*, *"Moestitiae Encomium"* has been described as further evidence
of Thompson's kinship with the Decadent writers of the 1890s, for it
"begins with a desolate picture of a fantasy landscape, clearly a reflec-
tion of laudanum sensations."[23] A monologue spoken in a marsh
eerily illuminated by "an unlawful moon," it records the world-weari-
ness familiar in fin de siècle literature: "Alas for the nineteenth century, with so much pleasure, and so little joy; so much learning, and
so little wisdom; so much effort, and so little fruition; so many phi-
losophers, and such little philosophy; so many seers, and such little
vision; so many prophets, and such little foresight; so many teachers,
and such an infinite wild vortex of doubt! the one divine thing left
to us is Sadness."[24] Like many of the poems written at Storrington,
"Moestitiae Encomium" may be seen as literary experimentation, testing
the symbolic and rhythmic resources of prose and producing a mood
picture or tone poem.

Because of the intoxicating verbal and metaphoric effects of
Thompson's poetry—and also because of his personal history—readers
associated him with the Aesthetic movement. Thompson, however,
dissociated himself from the literary and moral excesses of Aestheticism or Decadence. In 1897, for example, he changed publishers,
partly because of a dispute over royalties, but mostly because John
Lane published a "class of literature," "publications of which I disap-
prove," written by contributors to the *Yellow Book* and the *Savoy*.[25]

Thompson also opposed another artistic movement of the late nineteenth century, the Naturalism of Zola and his followers. An essay
called "The Error of the Extreme Realists," published in the June
1889 issue of *Merry England,* condemns Naturalism for wrongly emphasizing sensuality and ugliness. Instead of charging them with im-
morality, the refrain of other critics, Thompson maintained that
Naturalists falsified life by depicting an unnatural preponderance of
baseness.[26] Principally, however, he protested that in selecting repel-
lent material they ignored what in "Paganism Old and New" he defined as the chief goal of art—beauty: "art resides, not in
undiscerning comprehensiveness, but in discerning selection. Hence,
in order to condemn the methods of the ultra-realists there is no need

to invoke morality. . . . Zolaism is not artistic completeness: it is artistic excess" (*RP*, 210).

When Thompson wrote the early prose that dramatizes his criticisms of both Aestheticism and Naturalism, he was exceedingly mindful of the ugly side of life. He had recently experienced drug withdrawal, fortified by his religion and his aspirations for a poetic career. His personal knowledge of the joint importance of literature and religion as supports for the human spirit suggests why his prose so consistently argues the moral and philosophical basis of art. Perhaps also because of this experience, bodily and spiritual well-being became an important theme for Thompson, especially in his monograph "Health and Holiness," published in 1905 (completed in 1903) but developed from ideas he first discussed in a book review in *Merry England* in August 1891. The expanded version, his only prose published in book form during his life, is entitled "Health and Holiness: A Study of the Relations between Brother Ass, the Body, and His Rider, the Soul."

Based upon St. Francis of Assisi's image of the Body as an Ass ridden by the Soul, the work may be seen in the medieval tradition of debates between Body and Soul. The essay specifically denies that asceticism is necessary for sanctity, maintaining that physical vigor expresses and also nurtures spiritual vigor: "The body . . . is immersed in the soul, as a wick is dipped in oil; and its flame of active energy is increased or diminished by the strength or weakness of the . . . soul."[27] "Health and Holiness" expresses in more worldly terms ideas found in an essay "The Image of God," published in the *Franciscan Annals* of July 1893. Also alluding to St. Francis's image of Brother Ass, this earlier essay elaborates the theological premise that the human body was created in the image of God. Like many of Thompson's prose pieces, it features metaphors also employed in his poetry. For example, it depicts man as "a swinging-wicket between the material and immaterial universes, opening by his soul upon the angels, by his body upon the stars," an image used again in the poem "Any Saint" (1894).[28]

Descriptions of the contemporary world in "Health and Holiness," like the image in "Paganism Old and New" of the spiritually and aesthetically impoverished Victorians, tinge Thompson's moral and religious ideas with social criticism. Contrasting his contemporaries' lack of vigor with the Renaissance man's gusto—much as "Paganism Old and New" contrasts the aesthetic delight of the classical world with the industrial pall of the modern—Thompson in "Health and Holiness" draws a dispiriting picture: "we are too nervous, intricate, devitalized. We find our austerities ready-made. . . . The pride of life is no more; to live is itself an ascetic exercise; we require spurs to being, not a snaffle to rein back the ardour of being. Man is his own mortification. Hamlet has increased and multiplied, and his seed fill the land" (*Poems*, 3:254). Throughout Thompson's prose health of the individual body and of the social body reflect and nourish healthy spirits and healthy art.

The Poet's Vocabulary: Image and Symbol

Diagnosing one particular weakness in Dowson's Decadent verse, Thompson reiterated a complaint he also lodged against pagan poetry: the pitiable young poet had emulated "Greek artistry" by emphasizing "form and structure." Thompson, on the other hand, preferred the "Gothic or Celtic" style "rooted in a peculiar spiritual intimacy."[29] In an essay called "Form and Formalism" (1893) Thompson expounded his objections to the classical emphasis on discipline and patterning, developing ideas he had foreshadowed in "Paganism Old and New." Formalism stems from an analytical attitude basically inimical to the spontaneity, love, and beauty essential for poetry: "Many think in the head; but it is the thinking in the heart that is most wanted." In the arts and in life "Formalism is the repressor of vitality: therefore let us away with form."[30]

In this brief essay Thompson is concerned with philosophical and religious matters more than with literary theory, but in "The Way of Imperfection," published in the November 1889 *Merry England*, he stresses the value of literary individuality, variety, even character.[31] He contrasts the cold, classical worship of form and control with the vital English tradition that stems from the Goth (the "iconoclast" of perfection) and finds its "consummate product" in Shakespeare, "in whom greatness and imperfection reached their height."[32] Thompson criticizes contemporary artists because they strive for symmetry and precision in "cloying enervating harmonies, destitute of those stimulating contrasts by which the great colourists threw into relief the general agreement of their hues," or in the "love of miniature finish" which "leads to the tyranny" of sonnets, ballades, rondeaux, and other finely polished and constricting poetic forms popular in the late nineteenth century (*Poems*, 3:98). These comments suggest a theoretical basis for Thompson's own preference in most of his major poems for the ode form—though perhaps, because of the ode's flexibility in length of line and stanza, in rhyme scheme and meter, Thompson might have spoken of the ode's "formlessness."

"The Way of Imperfection" defends literary eccentricity and variety. Thompson attacks, for example, writers' reducing their characters to fit insipid patterns of the hero and heroine, especially the stereotyped "perfect woman." He also castigates dispassionate objectivity in characterization, when novelists "stand coldly aloof from their characters." Related to "the error of the extreme realists," this attempt to reproduce "Nature, uninterfered with by the writer's ideals or sympathies" is "fatal to artistic illusion," for characters so depicted "do not move us because they do not move" their creators (*Poems*, 3:101).

"The Way of Imperfection" justifies idiosyncracies or the "mannerisms" that constitute personal style: "The object of writing is to communicate individuality, the object of style adequately to embody that individuality." Variety and distinctive personality in style oppose the blandness and mediocrity of what Thompson calls "perfection": "Men will not drink distilled water; it is entirely pure and entirely insipid" (*Poems*, 3:102).[33] In a review of De Quincey's *Confessions of an English Opium Eater* written a decade after "The Way of Imperfection" Thompson reiterated this defense of imperfection. The obvious flaws in De Quincey's style—"disproportionate, voluble, divagating, exasperating, tedious, insistent upon the infinitely little"—help to make the work a masterpiece. "It is a monument of personality, triumphant over all defects issuing from that personality."[34] The spirited defense of eccentricity in "The Way of Imperfection" and later book reviews supplies theoretical grounds for Thompson's own audacious poetic style.

Another essay, never published by Thompson, enunciates a related literary principle also pertinent to his own poetry. "*Anima Simplicitatis*" explains that simplicity, which is not antithetical to complexity, "is nothing else than the perfect coordination of parts, working effortlessly together towards a single and unitive result." What people call complexity is frequently merely "disintegration."[35] In light of critics' charges that Thompson often amassed images and verbal effects without sufficient coherence or purpose, his elaboration of this principle of literary simplicity is particularly significant. Most readers, he held, think simplicity is merely "direct language." If a poet relies heavily on imagery, especially "what we call 'remote' [imagery], he is thought to err against simplicity. Now if he do so merely for beautiful adornment, the criticism is just; but if he do so for needs of expression, unjust" (*RRLS*, 315).

Most important, because the true poet often seeks to communicate truths of a higher plane, beyond the ordinary and therefore beyond the compass of familiar vocabulary, he must necessarily rely on image to suggest his meanings. In contrast to the philosopher and theologian, who painstakingly define new terminology for their audience, the poet uses imagery that "unlike words, is self-revealing to those who possess the requisite pre-perceptions" (*RRLS*, 317). In fact, words—which are usually analytical and strive for exclusive meaning—often cannot express the poet's perceptions, for he deals in synthesis and analogy. "The very fact that a word has a defined and universally accepted meaning appropriated to some perception on the daily plane, makes it an unfit sign for a new perception" (*RRLS*, 316). *"Anima Simplicitatis"* asserts that both imagery, which expresses truths that readers cannot ordinarily apprehend, and unconventional diction, which similarly suggests the ineffable or interprets the enigmatic, are "entirely needful for expression," are in fact a poet's "direct language" (*RRLS*, 315).

Thompson also defended symbolism as a necessary feature of a poet's language. In a manuscript fragment called "Analogies Between God, Nature, Man and the Poet," written some time before June 1893, he observed that "a poet is born with the instinctive sense of veritable correspondences hidden from the multitude."[36] To communicate these truths, he "is driven to express his perceptions through the shrouded language of symbolism" partly by the exigencies of a language that cannot sufficiently embody them, and partly by the example of the symbolic world, which the poet in turn interprets to readers through his own symbols: "Man is a symbol, Nature a metaphor, heaven and earth are written in hieroglyphs. The universe is a metonymy for God. It is a labyrinth, with God for center, and the *gnothi seauton* as its clue. The poet, therefore is Nature's alchemist. . . . few realise how much which is regarded as mere fanciful imagery expresses secret identities of essence in outwardly separate provinces of being" (*RRLS*, 347). Thompson's emphasis on symbols in the poetic vocabulary clearly depends on his view, the essence of Christian Platonism, that the physical universe symbolizes God.[37] As one who deciphers the symbols of God for his fellow man, and then himself creates verbal symbols, the poet reflects the creative activities of God. In terms of literary practice, his view of the function of symbols relates Thompson to the French Symbolists (as illustrated in his poems "The Nightmare of the Witch-Babies" and "The Owl") and to early twentieth-century Imagists (as in "Lover's Progress" and "The Bird"). His ideas of the poet resemble Coleridge's, though Thompson took specific exception to the Romantic theorist's definitions of *fancy* and *imagination*, at least as Coleridge was interpreted by Leigh Hunt: "inward resemblance may be as superficial as outward resemblance, and it is then the product of *fancy*, or fantasy. When the resemblance is more than rooted in the hidden nature of things, its discernment is the product of imagination. This is the real distinction; fancy detects resemblances, imagination identities."[38]

The Idea of the Poet

Although not specifically concerned with poetic symbolism, Thompson's best-known essay, "Shelley," elaborates his concept of the poet. Probably begun in September 1889 during his rigorous drug withdrawal at Storrington, "Shelley" occupied him, he wrote, for "three painful months."[39] He seems to have spent even longer, revising extensively, for he announced to Wilfrid Meynell that he had forced himself to let it go in February 1890: "Seemed to me dreadful trash when I read it over before sending it. Shut my eyes and ran to the post, or some demon might have set me to work unpicking it again."[40] This "dreadful trash" remained unpublished until the year after Thompson's death, 1908, but when it finally appeared in the *Dublin Review*, which had rejected it almost twenty years earlier, the journal sold out immediately and required a second printing. The second issue was introduced by a letter from George Wyndham calling it "the most important contribution to pure Letters written in English during the last twenty years." In passing this judgment, Wyndham declared, he compared the essay not only with prose criticism but with poetry as well.[41]

The project was especially important to Thompson, both as homage to his beloved Shelley and as serious work that tested his resources and also gave him purpose during his recovery from addiction: it "might have been written in tears, and is proportionately dear to me." Yet he was sufficiently objective to predict two reasons why the *Dublin Review* might refuse to print it. First, it was "written at an almost incessant level of poetic prose, and seethes with imagery like my poetry itself."[42] Hardly a flaw, this opulent imagery provides numerous enchanting and memorable passages, as for example, the description of Shelley's imagination and childlike sense of wonder: "His playthings are those which the gods give their children. The universe is his box of toys. . . . He is gold-dusty with tumbling amidst the stars. He makes bright mischief with the moon. The meteors nuzzle their noses in his hand. . . . He dances in and out of the gates of heaven: its floor is littered with his broken fancies."[43] Parallels between this prose description of Shelley at play and the verse depiction of youth in "An Anthem of Earth" (written in 1894) illustrate the affinities between what Thompson called his "prose-poetry" (He declared, "I recollect nothing like it in English prose")[44] and his actual poetry. The torrent of felicitous images in "Shelley" forces readers to apply Thompson's appreciation of Shelley's metaphoric inventiveness to Thompson himself.

The second objection to "Shelley" that Thompson anticipated would keep the essay out of print is that it begins with "a fiery attack on Catholic Philistinism."[45] As in "Paganism Old and New" Thompson was attempting to rehabilitate Shelley the poet, who had been frequently denigrated by readers disturbed by Shelley the notorious atheist and moral renegade. In delineating Thompson's view of the poet he had most studied the essay also illustrates his studied view of the Poet.

Reiterating an idea important in his first published essay, Thompson argues that doctrinal matters remain largely irrelevant to evaluations of a poet. Because the artist's main objective is to create beauty, he achieves much the same goal as that of the Church. The poet thus ministers to mankind's needs much as a priest does: "With many the religion of beauty must always be a passion and a power . . . it is only evil when divorced from the worship of the Primal Beauty. Poetry is the preacher to men of the earthly as you [the clergy and pious laity] of the Heavenly Fairness; . . . you praise the Creator for His works, and [Beauty] shows you that they are very good" (*Poems,* 3:2).

Shelley demonstrated the fairness of creation through his fresh, spontaneous, childlike (though not childish) perceptions. To be a child, perceiving the world with wonderment and imagination, is "to believe in love, to believe in loveliness, to believe in belief; it is to be so little that the elves can reach to whisper in your ear . . . it is to live in a nutshell and to count yourself the king of infinite space"

(*Poems*, 3:7). Like Shelley, poets must have a "child's faculty of make-believe raised to the nth power" (*Poems*, 3:18).

This special faculty doubtless contributes to the poet's isolation from his fellows: "Most poets, probably, like most saints, are prepared for their mission by an initial segregation, as the seed is buried to germinate: before they can utter the oracle of poetry, they must first be divided from the body of men. It is the severed head that makes the seraph" (*Poems*, 3:11). Biographers have often applied Thompson's view of Shelley's isolation, especially a passage that suggests he was tormented at school, to Thompson himself, though recollections of those who knew him as a youth do not corroborate this painful image. As the phrase "like most saints" implies, his remarks about isolation relate more directly to his view of the poet as a sanctified mediator between mankind and higher Truth, Beauty, and God.

His association of poet and saint led Thompson to infer from Shelley's poetry that had he lived longer, the Romantic rebel would doubtless have become a Christian; Shelley's "rise" from atheism to pantheism marked but a stage in a refining maturation. Thompson refuted criticisms of Shelley that were based on moral grounds: "We do not believe that a truly corrupted spirit can write consistently ethereal poetry." Moreover, "the devil can do many things. But the devil cannot write poetry. He may mar a poet, but he cannot make a poet" (*Poems*, 3:33).

The idea of the poet's kinship to the saint took deep root in Thompson's thought. His allegorical poem "The Mistress of Vision" (published in 1897) develops the image of the poet as a secular counterpart of the saint, and the idea also permeates his prose. "A Modern Study of Sanctity," for example, a review published in 1898, remarks that the "faculties native in the poet are the natural basis of what is called contemplation in the saint."[46] The analogy remained intact in Thompson's late prose as well. In "Health and Holiness" he elaborates on the "parallelisms between the psychology of the Saints and the psychology of men of genius,—parallelisms which . . . are specially observable where the genius is of the poetic or artistic kind, in the broad sense of the word 'artistic' ": "Both Saint and Poet undergo a preparation for their work . . . a process of pain and struggle. For [the Poet] it is nothing else than a gradual conformation to artistic law. . . . he is himself absorbed into the law, moulded to it, until he becomes sensitively respondent to its faintest motion, as the spiritualized body to the soul. Thenceforth he needs no guidance from for-

mal rule, having a more delicate rule within him. . . . In like
manner does the Saint receive into himself and become one with divine law. . . .[47]

Thompson not only discussed his favorite poets in terms of the
spirituality of saints, but also discussed the literary accomplishments
of saints such as Augustine, Francis of Assisi, Francis de Sales, and
John of the Cross. As he commented in "Health and Holiness," "The
energy of the saints has left everywhere its dents upon the world. . . .
Take, if you will, poetry. In the facile forefront of lyric sublimity
stand the Hebrew prophets" (*Poems*, 3:277). Thompson also commended the prophets as poets in book reviews, as in an 1898 review
of the poetically accomplished writings of Ezekiel.[48] He summarized
his view of poet as saint and saint as poet in the essay "Form and
Formalism," which essentially defends the life of religious orders: "a
great poet, . . . who is likewise a great thinker, does for truth what
Christ did for God, the Supreme Truth."[49]

Thompson did not always describe the poet so reverentially, however. "A Renegade Poet on the Poet" (1892), for example, defends
the usefulness of poetry in an age that remained at heart ruthlessly
utilitarian. But this defense of the arts wittily portrays the poet as
one "who endeavours to make the worst of both worlds. For he is
thought seldom to make provision for himself in the next life, and
'tis odds if he gets any in this." In a similarly satiric manner Thompson predicts that if most other men go to Hell, the poet will not,
"for 'tis inconceivable he should ever do as other men."

Throughout the essay Thompson comically uses as his bête noire
Robert Louis Stevenson, who had argued that the writer is but "a
poor devil of a fellow, who lives to please, and earns his bread by
doing what he likes"—and who should, therefore, feel humble before
men who do something useful.[50] Thompson counters that there is
"utility in pleasure . . . when it makes a man's heart the better for
it; as do, I am very certain, sun, and flowers, and Stevensons" (*Poems*,
3:107).

Despite this flippant manner, Thompson seriously defends poetry
as "the teacher of beauty; and without beauty men would soon lose
the conception of a God" (*Poems*, 3:106). The concluding definition
of the poet combines the comic spirit which permeates the essay with
sober reflections on the poet's isolation. Unlike the several works that
suggest the poet, like the saint, is set apart by his sanctity, "A Renegade Poet on the Poet" describes an artist isolated and exploited by an

unappreciative and unsympathetic public: "The poor fool . . . devotes assiduous practice to acquiring an art which comes least natural to him of all men; and, after employing a world of pains to scorn the world, is strangely huffed that it should return the compliment in kind." Having been taught to flee the world for the sake of his art, the poet resembles operatic eunuchs who are severed from their kind to gratify the ear of their audience, as the poet is isolated to "gratify their understanding" (*Poems*, 3:108–9).

The celebration of the poet in the "Shelley" essay echoes specific details of Thompson's theory of poetic diction and imagery articulated in such works as "Form and Formalism" and "The Way of Imperfection." Often he posits his theory by discussing the shortcomings of contemporary poetic practice. When compared to the dynamic poetry of Shelley and his contemporaries, late nineteenth-century poetry "is mildewed" because of one major defect—"the predominance of art over inspiration, of body over soul" ("Shelley," *Poems*, 3:4). This flaw manifests itself in excessive deliberation in choosing words which "results in loss of spontaneity." Thompson also complains of "the habit of always taking the most ornate word, the word most removed from ordinary speech" (5). "The literary revolution against the despotic diction of [Alexander] Pope seems issuing, like political revolutions, in a despotism of its own making (6).[51] These factors have produced a poetic diction that is rather like "a kaleidoscope, and one's chief curiosity is as to the precise combinations into which the pieces will be shifted" (5).

In a note to the "Shelley" essay Thompson suggests that the poet can avoid recurring to an "exclusive coterie of poetic words" or "aristocratic circle of language" by occasionally writing prose. This practice should "maintain fresh and comprehensive a poet's diction" by "keeping him in touch with the great commonality, the proletariat of speech. For it is with words as with men: constant intermarriage within the limits of a patrician clan begets effete refinement; and to reinvigorate the stock, its veins must be replenished from hardy plebeian blood" (5–6).

Although Thompson rarely used what we might call "plebeian" or prosaic language, he was aware that his own predilection for neologisms and archaisms could constitute a defect in poetry.[52] Even so, he defended the use of archaic forms or word coinages as means of enriching the predictable poetic diction of his age, and also of expressing meaning more precisely. In a book review of 1902, for example, he

indicated why a writer might purposefully choose archaisms and
neologisms by defending both Thomas Carlyle's revival of the archaic
swinkt and Shakespeare's coinage *soud* for the onomatopoeic effect of
the old and new words.[53] Such comments, coupled with his complaint
against the predictability of late nineteenth-century diction, put his
own eccentric use of language into a special perspective. Whatever we
may say about the "artificiality" of his language, its variance from the
common usages of his day keeps it from being "artificial" as he applied the term to his contemporaries: "nothing is so artificial as our
simplicity. . . . We are self-conscious to the finger-tips."[54] Thompson once explained that his own diction, though it smacked of the
seventeenth century to his readers, had grown natural to him in his
boyhood. He described an occasion when he was seven and his mother
admonished him, "you have read Shakespeare so much that you are
beginning to talk Shakespeare without knowing it. You must take
care, or people will think you odd." Thompson insisted that his
quaint or startling poetic diction was "often as unconscious as that
childish Elizabethanism uttered in my little nightgown."[55] And in
truth, even his most apparently contrived diction seems in his best
poetry to be remarkably unself-conscious.

Concerning imagery, the "Shelley" essay also reiterates theory discussed in his other prose, suggesting that imagery is the most apparent manifestation of a poet's spontaneity and inventiveness, of the
"imperfection" that Thompson judged infinitely superior to "form."
His comments on Shelley insistently point to Thompson himself: "It
would have been as conscious an effort for him to speak without figure
as it is for most men to speak with figure. Suspended in the dripping
well of his imagination the commonest object becomes encrusted with
imagery" (*Poems*, 3:20). Virtually all commentators acknowledge the
resourcefulness and effectiveness of Thompson's image-making, but as
he expressed familiar criticisms, "I accumulated imagery until I became obscure and inartistic." He candidly described the chief flaw in
his least successful work when he solicited the Meynells' evaluation of
Sister Songs: "do not suffer me to think that I have wrought a beautiful
bracelet . . . merely because you never saw so many jewels set in the
same space before."[56]

In the "Shelley" essay Thompson defends metaphoric amplitude by
emphasizing that beauty is the sole object of true poetry, and the
greatest poetic beauty arises from imagery. He was pleased when one
critic, while confirming Thompson's weakness of piling images to ex-

cess, exclaimed "but what a splendid fault! And your imagery is often so unexpected and surprising."[57] As the evaluation of Shelley demonstrates, Thompson prized exactly this "splendid fault" in other poets. Shelley, he wrote, continued the tradition of the seventeenth-century Metaphysical poets stemming from Crashaw who "loved imagery for its own sake" and stressed "how beautiful a thing the frank toying with imagery may be. . . . It is only evil when the poet, on the straight way to a fixed object, lags continually from the path to play. This is commendable neither in poet nor errand-boy" (*Poems*, 3:21). This trivializing or "toying" does not occur, Thompson judges, when the figurative language stems from "passionate spontaneity" rather than contrivance. His "Shelley" essay and poems such as "A Corymbus for Autumn" or "An Anthem of Earth" confirm the splendor possible in metaphoric extravagance.

In connection with these comments on poetic imagery Thompson discusses poetic treatments of Nature, taking issue with Wordsworth on the need for factual fidelity in landscape portraiture. With Nature, Thompson held, Wordsworth and his followers "will admit no tampering: they exact the direct interpretive reproduction of her; that the poet should follow her as a mistress, not use her as a handmaid." Shelley, in contrast, considered Nature "not a picture set for his copying, but a palette set for his brush; not a habitation prepared for his inhabiting, but a Coliseum whence he might quarry stones for his own palaces." "Instead of culling Nature," Shelley "crossed with its pollen the blossoms of his own soul" (*Poems*, 3:19, 20).

This praise of Shelley's imaginative play with the raw materials found in Nature does not mean that Thompson counseled poets to disregard physical actuality. He suggested in a book review of 1901 that writers should enrich their works with the findings of modern science. Among poets, however, Tennyson "is almost alone" in using the theme of the extinction of species. Thompson observed that contemporary novelists, at least, should mine "this romance of the young earth."[58] In "Health and Holiness" he argued that scientific findings, when properly understood, demonstrate "the commerce between body and spirit," acting as "the witness and handmaid of theology."[59] But he also recognized that the poet might have difficulty accommodating scientific principles to poetic uses, for reasons related to his premise that poets must speak through symbol and image: "A scientific fact must have become popularised before it can be used allusively without obscurity to the general reader: . . . poetry is an art of allusion and pregnant statement, not of analysis: the poet who explains is lost. For this reason science seems even more impracticable as the ground-work of poetry."[60]

In his own poetry Thompson turned familiar scientific phenomena to fanciful use, remaining faithful both to analytical fact and to imaginative interpretation. Offended once when Alice Meynell questioned his Nature detail, he patronizingly explained that his observations on flowers that open at night were accurate, as "Surely anyone who knows a forest from a flower-pot is aware." Like so many of his essays, this jocular letter mixes his ideas about Nature, art, and love, and seasons them with a dash of social criticism: "I sometimes wonder whether the best of you Londoners do not regard Nature as a fine piece of the Newlyn school, kindly lent by the Almighty for public exhibition. Few seem to realize that she is alive, has almost as many ways as a woman, and is to be lived with, not merely looked at." He objected that even rural dwellers trivialized Nature by viewing her as a collection of "splendid" views. "I protest against Nature being regarded as on view. If a man told me to take a three-quarter view of the woman I loved, because I should find her a fine composition; I fear I should incline to kick him extremely, and ask whether he thought her five-foot-odd of canvas . . . having companioned Nature in her bed-chamber no less than her presence-room, what I write of her is not lightly to be altered."[61]

Platonic "Shadowings" of Truth

Thompson's humorous defense of his intimacy with Nature relates to an idea he pursued quite seriously in an essay published in the February 1890 issue of *Merry England,* "Nature's Immortality." The essay, written like "Shelley" in his highly metaphoric "prose-poetry," discusses Nature's relationship to God. Refuting the concept, which he attributes to Romantic pantheists (particularly Wordsworth and Shelley), of Nature as a sentient entity, Thompson declares that Nature is unresponsive to human moods: "Absolute Nature lives not in our life, nor yet is lifeless, but lives in the life of God: and in so far, and so far merely, as man himself lives in that life, does he come into sympathy with Nature, and Nature with him. She is God's daughter, who stretches her hand only to her Father's friends."[62] Even though he here employs an anthropomorphic image, Thompson rejects the sentimentalizing tendency to portray Nature as a being who responds sympathetically to humanity. Nor does he espouse the Platonic notion passed through the Romantics that Nature is "a veil concealing the Eternal, . . . which we must rend to behold that Face" (*Poems*, 3:82–83).

Thompson specifically Christianizes Platonic thought, declaring that "Earthly beauty is but heavenly beauty taking to itself flesh. Yet, though this objective presentment of the Divine Ideal be relatively more perfect than any human presentment of a human ideal, though it be the most flawless of possible embodiments; yet is even the Divine embodiment transcendently inferior to the Divine Ideal." Because Nature is part of the Divine Ideal, the woods, streams, meads, hills, and seas all exist permanently. We will not cease to see the beauty of Nature when we enter the beauty of Heaven, for "in Heaven is earth" (*Poems*, 3:87).

This brief essay commands interest because it demonstrates Thompson's method of "endeavouring analogically to *suggest* an idea." He was "not trying to *explain* anything, metaphysically or otherwise," merely creating "a fantasy, which the writer likes to think may be a dim shadowing of truth" (*Poems*, 3:86). These comments, especially the figure of dimly shadowing truth, suggest his indebtedness to Platonic thought as well as to Plato's technique of conveying truths through analogies. Like "Analogies Between God, Nature, Man and the Poet," this essay suggests that the poet's activity is tantamount to entering the mind of God to re-create Ideal Beauty. Thompson explains three distinct stages in an artist's creative process: recognizing the ideal; conceiving a mental image of the ideal; and finally reproducing this mental image in an external, objective form.

Although it has not been discussed in these terms, the essay called "The Fourth Order of Humanity" (1891) may similarly be read as an endeavor "analogically to suggest" a Platonic ideal. It elaborates thoughts about Beauty, which in "Nature's Immortality" Thompson calls a "trinity" comprising Poetry, Art, and Music. Commentators have primarily discussed "The Fourth Order of Humanity" in terms of autobiographical significance, taking the essay as evidence that Thompson as a child liked to play with dolls, and later as a reluctant medical student spent entire days worshipping a bust of the Vatican Melpomene in a Manchester gallery, thereby demonstrating his imagination and his preference for art and idealized images of women to real human beings.[63]

Actually the whimsical depiction of dolls as a "fourth order of humanity" may be read as an illustration of Platonic ideas of Beauty and Love, written in a relaxed manner akin to the style of Charles Lamb's personal essays. The dolls of the narrator's sisters and the statue of Melpomene symbolize permanent and idealized beauty far superior to the flawed beauty of real women, who use artificial cosmetics, wigs, and padding to achieve a meretricious imitation of the permanent beauty "natural" to dolls and sculpture. Unlike these copyists, the narrator worshipped the ideal beauty of dolls: "I fell in love with them; I did not father them."[64]

When he matured from his desire to nurture human "imitations" of dolls (by holding infants), to an attitude of worship, the narrator became aware that even art embodied the essence of Beauty only imperfectly—the bust of Melpomene had an asymmetrical mouth. The speaker thus learned that human beings and their artistic devisings emulate, but never fully actualize, the idea of Beauty in the world of forms. Moreover, his reverence for Beauty has conducted him to Love, and as a lover of the Ideal, he may be seen as having entered a "fourth order of humanity," beyond ordinary men, women, and children. Seen in this light the essay is hardly a trivial autobiographical document. Instead it shows Thompson's gift for employing the most mundane experiences to symbolic effect, and for conveying his philosophical and aesthetic Platonism in deceptively simple, familiar vehicles.

At the conclusion of the essay the speaker rejects the "vain fable that the ambrosial" bust of Melpomene was "really an unspiritual compound of lime, which the gross ignorant call plaster of Paris." Those less grossly ignorant recognize the image as an enchanted and enchanting embodiment of Beauty. "If Paris indeed had to do with her, it was he of Ida," famed for loving beauty unmatched by all the goddesses of Olympus (*Poems*, 3:70). From the arresting beginning to this last witty pun, "The Fourth Order of Humanity" is one of Thompson's cleverest prose pieces.

Satire and Social Criticism

Like many of the essays primarily concerned with topics such as aesthetic theory or the life of religious orders, "The Fourth Order of Humanity" incorporates bits of effective social satire. It darts satiric glances not only at women's painting themselves like dolls, but also at children's destructive and fairly sadistic treatment of dolls and at stereotypical sex roles that prohibited boys from holding infants or loving dolls. Like this last implicit criticism of prevailing mores,

Thompson's satire frequently attacks the social code, as in his comment in the "Shelley" essay that the increasing facility of divorce must produce an era "when the young lady in reduced circumstances will no longer turn governess, but will be open to engagement as wife at a reasonable stipend."[65]

Most often, Thompson satirized the temper of the age—stuffy, insensitive, stultifying. He often attacked utilitarianism, especially for its inadequate valuation of the arts, as when he observed that "if necessity be any criterion of usefulness . . ., the universal practice of mankind will prove poetry to be more useful than soap; since there is no recorded age in which men did not use poetry, but for some odd thousand years the world got on very tolerably well without soap."[66]

His most vivid and disturbing social criticism sheds this wryly satiric tone, however. His early review of *In Darkest England and the Way Out,* a study of the impoverished class written by the leader of the Salvation Army, General William Booth, appeared in *Merry England* for January 1891. Entitled "Catholics in Darkest England," the essay vividly contrasts the two Englands, demanding that the rich mount militant assistance for the poor. Attributing the plight of the poor to the cult of individualism in British economic and social practices, Thompson labels the doctrine of individualism "the script of selfishness, . . . the maxim of Cain."[67] Echoing Tennyson, he admonishes that concern for the self has allowed to flourish "unchecked the rehatched 'dragons of the prime' " (*Poems,* 3:61). The essay shows another facet of Thompson's richly variable prose style, for the warm geniality of "The Fourth Order of Humanity" and the heady imagery of "Shelley" here give way to an incantatory rhythm of parallel constructions and impassioned metaphors. Despite his strictures against depicting ugliness in the manner of "the extreme realists," Thompson draws a chilling portrait of life in the London streets, which he himself knew too well. One especially moving scene (a passage omitted when Wilfrid Meynell reprinted the essay in his edition of *Poems and Essays*) describes derelicts seeking admittance to shelters provided by the Salvation Army and the Catholic Church: "The nightly crowd of haggard men . . . the anxious waiting while the ticket-holders are slowly admitted; the thrill—the almost shudder—through the crowd when the manager emerges to pick out men for the vacant beds left over after the ticket-holders' admission, the sickening suspense and fear in all the eyes as—choosing a man here and there—he passes along the huddled ranks."[68] Thompson's recollections of homeless

poverty loom just as vivid and terrible in a dejected letter he wrote
nearly a decade later, probably in July 1900: "The very streets weigh
upon me. These horrible streets, with their gangrenous multitudes,
blackening ever into lower mortifications of humanity! The brute
men; these lads who have almost lost the faculty of human speech,
who howl & growl like animals, or use a tongue which is itself a cancerous disintegration of speech: these girls whose practice is a putrid
ulceration of love, venting foul and purulent discharge—for their very
utterance is hideous blasphemy against the sacrosanctity of lovers' language!"[69]

Like the essay "In Darkest England," this letter describing "the
fumes of congregated evil, the herded effluence from millions of fes-
tering souls," suggests the power that must have characterized a
longer prose work Thompson projected on the subject of London
street life. In the spring of 1897 he promised his publisher a volume
that in pictures and commentary would contrast "Fair London" with
"Terrible London." His detailed description of the project focused especially on the terrible aspects of the city—"weird, sordid and
gloomy"—those aspects "evident to a houseless wanderer" between
midnight and dawn, "for which my own experiences furnish me with
material." He wanted particularly to "dwell on . . . the *character*—of
horror, sombreness, weirdness, or beauty—of various scenes. My own
mind turns especially towards the gloomier majesties . . . of London,
because I have seen it most peculiarly under those circumstances."[70]

Well qualified for writing such a book by both his firsthand knowledge of its subject and his verbal power, Thompson never delivered
the manuscript, even though it had already been announced in the
Academy.[71] In February 1901, however, he completed an article on the
same subject.[72] Designed for publication in the *Nineteenth Century,* the
the article never appeared and the manuscript has not been found. It
is possible that Wilfrid Meynell, always eager to purge from the
poet's image hints of his dereliction and drug addiction, persuaded
Thompson to suppress the work.

Unlike his intense descriptions of street life, most of Thompson's
social criticism reveals resourceful wit and a pervasive irony. Besides
the occasional satiric barb embedded in essays on literary and philosophical topics and, frequently, in his book reviews, Thompson's satiric bent produced works such as the unpublished manuscript called
"Modern Men: the Devil." Described as a "fresh article" in a draft of
a letter to William Ernest Henley, editor of the *National Observer,* in

early 1891, the essay was not printed and may never have been sent.[73] Suggesting that modern social ills manifest the devil's spirit, Thompson in the essay dances nimbly over such subjects as industrialists' exploitation of cheap labor and the commonplace practice of sacrificing personal integrity for financial advancement, as well as swearing, poetasters, the Royal Academy, the contemporary stage, the public, "bad French books, and . . . worse English criticisms of them," and various individual painters and poets. All these blights on civilization Thompson wittily attributes to the devil: "though God, we confess, may be a little out of fashion in these times, the Devil keeps the vogue in a surprising manner." But, he quips in closing, though the devil is responsible "for all which offends the British Matron," "he has some saving conscience—he is not responsible for the British Matron."[74] In a late review (1905) of Samuel Butler's *Hudibras* Thompson declared, "Perhaps to blame a satirist for uncharitableness is like finding fault with a tiger for inhumanity, or with Rabelais for grossness."[75] Though not primarily a satirist, Thompson nevertheless demonstrated that successful satire need be neither inhuman nor gross.

Dramatic Experiments

His talent for satire supplies the interest in his attempts as a dramatist. Early in his writing career, in the fall of 1891, he attempted a comedy entitled *Venus' Fly-Trap*. It satirizes contemporary literature, partly drawing on Thompson's sole visit, in late 1891, to a meeting of the Rhymers' Club, a writers' club which met in London in the early 1890s. When Thompson sent the first scene to Alice Meynell in December, he described his satiric purposes, remarking that he had included "glorified 'Rhymers,' " only one of whom bore "any relation to the original." He directed his sharpest satire at "the more conspicuous defects of my own earlier poetry."[76] One passage may be seen to express his own disappointment at not having won an audience beyond Catholic circles.[77]

When in 1897 he embarked on his "new life" as a journalist and sought new sources of income through expanded literary activities, he seems to have returned to the idea of writing plays. In late 1897 and 1898 he wrote two brief dramas, *Napoleon Judges* and *Man Proposes, But Woman Disposes*, and began a third, *Saul*, which exists only in a very rough manuscript.[78] That Thompson should have considered writing for the stage seems odd, for neither his letters nor the mem-

oirs of his acquaintances record his having any great interest in contemporary theater.[79] References in his notebooks and one of his plays
indicate that Thompson knew the work of Ibsen, and his voluminous
reading, especially in recent literature, makes it likely that he had
read and doubtless heard much about contemporary plays even if he
did not see them performed.

Nearly three years after he began work on *Napoleon Judges* he "summoned up pluck to send my little play" to the critic William Archer,
who had favorably reviewed *New Poems* in 1897, "asking him whether
it afforded any encouragement to serious study of writing for the
stage." Archer answered no, though as Thompson phrased it, "he
cautiously refrains from a precise negative." This criticism ended
Thompson's thoughts of writing for the stage, yet he still wanted to
read the Meynells his "chucked-up *Saul*," "a frankly closet-play" and
therefore "beyond the range of Archer."[80]

The evidence of his two completed plays shows that Thompson was
right in thinking that he would succeed better with closet drama.
Napoleon Judges and *Man Proposes, But Woman Disposes,* both two-scene
playlets, differ considerably. The first, a tragedy evidently intended
for staging, has no distinction whatever. It depicts Napoleon's judgment on one of his generals, who at a drunken banquet entertained
his mistress, an opera-dancer, by having one of his men, a convicted
deserter, shot. Napoleon arrives just in time to see this travesty of a
military execution and condemns the general to death for his breach
of military and moral codes. When the general's mistress is accidentally shot while trying to offer herself in place of her lover, Napoleon
recognizes her nobility.[81] The insipid romantic melodrama deserved to
be rejected when Thompson sent it in 1903 to *T. P.'s Weekly.*[82]

Man Proposes, But Woman Disposes, a "modern comedy, full of laboriously smart give and take," succeeds somewhat better.[83] The stage
directions that provide interpretive commentary ("A frightful interregnum of cold perspiration," or "One of those little scandals which
the most unexceptionable ladies seem to like best") and the satiric
footnotes suggest that the play was intended to be read, as does the
descriptive subtitle, *"Un conte sans Raconteur."* The drama resembles
the drawing-room comedies of the day, especially the comedy of manners so masterfully represented by Oscar Wilde's *The Importance of Being Earnest* (1895).

Though scarcely comparable to Wilde's standard, Thompson's
playlet offers two interesting features in the familiar situation of a
clever woman's manipulating a match between a young couple, both

of whom think they love someone else. The antiromantic resolution is quietly disturbing. After he proposes to Miss Black, Mr. Mortimer marvels, "A fellow doesn't really *know* how much he is in love with a girl until he tries!," revealing that "love" is no more than mild interest kindled by the lady's supposed interest in him. Miss Black's final recognition is equally antiromantic. Having been rejected by the man she thinks she loves, she accepts Mr. Mortimer instead: "I can be pretty happy with any decent good fellow. It's a very comfortable state of mind—not heroic but comfortable." Thompson avoids a formulaic ending even while employing romance formulas.

The witty dialogue provides the comedy's chief distinction. The satiric spirit permeates even the list of characters, where Thompson connects the females with the satire of women in Alexander Pope's *Epistle to a Lady*. Later he associates his male protagonist with Falstaff in a soliloquy by which Mortimer tries to persuade himself that discreet flight from the field of battle between the sexes might indeed be valorous. Throughout the play the superbly articulate characters reduce complex ethical issues into witty, well-turned phrases. The topics of satire include stereotyped sex roles ("any girl may talk about Plato, provided she hasn't read him"), Gladstone, the vogue for the Pre-Raphaelites, and the Higher Criticism.

As in the early *Venus' Fly-Trap*, Thompson satirizes the poet in the ladies' descriptions of a suitor who writes love poems to Miss Black. She fears that the poet does not feel the passion he writes: "I don't mind discovering that he is an empty attic; but I dislike having to go up so many stairs to it." Thompson, damned and praised for his plentiful imagery, is particularly puckish in satirizing a poet's metaphoric gift as a putrefaction: "your sun is your only breeder of metaphors; he breeds them out of your poet like flies out of carrion. You lay your poet out in a hot July day, and he is soon a corrupt mass of imagery; he crawls with similitudes, and taints the neighbourhood with ill-smelling fancy." Although Thompson's situation and characters merit no notice, his witty repartee is worthy of immensely entertaining comedy.

Critical Perspectives

The satire and irony that frequently enliven Thompson's book reviews succeed precisely because he had something of substance to say. Most of his readable, professional reviews were specifically literary— he evaluated volumes of poetry, anthologies, biographies, and studies of writers. But a sampling of his subjects reveals considerable versatility. He reviewed biographies of a Polish queen, Roman empresses, mystics and saints; letters of Napoleon and of Eloise and Abelard; a study of Burma and a book on prehistoric monsters. In literature his scope was even more impressive. He wrote about the *Niebelungenlied* and *Don Quixote,* the literary traditions of India, and the nursery rhymes of France. He analyzed poetry, drama, fiction, and essays. Regardless of the subject, the best essays—and even a rigorous assessment would rate a large proportion of his total output very highly— are judicious and persuasive. They offer consistently interesting *aperçus* in a flexible, engaging style—lively, witty, capable of forceful directness and of diplomatic indirection, of dramatic terseness and welcome amplification. In the reviews he effectively husbands the image-making talents sometimes used more prodigally in his other writing, and the reviewer's metaphors are as resourceful, apt, and memorable as the poet's.

His judgments on contemporary trends are almost invariably sound. He recognized that in the 1880s and 1890s American verse was "for the most part very respectable magazine-stuff, and no more." He complained that most American poets either "Whitmanise on the one hand, or follow the outworn Tennysonian convention on the other."[84] His praise of Madison Cawein and John Bannister Tabb seems understandable in an age when Emily Dickinson, whose works were just being published, attracted virtually no attention from British readers, and the likes of E. C. Stedman and Richard Hovey were as good as America had to offer.[85] Thompson evaluated poets of the Irish Revival with equal authority. While he recognized the passion and national color of the lesser Irish writers, he noted that their patriotic self-consciousness often overwhelmed their artistry. And he judged the young William Butler Yeats potentially superb.[86]

In British literature Thompson concentrated mostly on the two periods most native to him, the nineteenth century and the seventeenth, the latter the period most congenial to Thompson's own poetic style. As a reviewer he sampled widely among the editions, biographies, and studies of Wordsworth, Coleridge, Byron, Shelley, Keats, De Quincey, Carlyle, Landor, Mill, Tennyson, the Brownings, Ruskin, Rossetti, Morris, Swinburne, Patmore, Meredith, James Thomson, William Ernest Henley, A. E. Housman, and Robert Bridges. He also reviewed such relatively "minor" contemporaries as F. B. Money-Coutts, Sir Alfred Douglas, William Watson, Wilfrid Blunt,

Thomas Edward Brown, Arabella Shore, and Alice Meynell. This last name on the list of minor writers should suggest that Thompson's judgment of his contemporaries' importance did not always coincide with a later twentieth-century assessment, for he consistently ranked Alice Meynell among the first poets of the century.

His personal prejudices taint his literary judgments surprisingly little, however. When he was smarting from what he felt to be harsh reviews of the 1897 *New Poems*, Thompson protested "how powerfully people's views (theological, philosophical or otherwise) influenced their attitude toward contemporary poetry."[87] A survey of his reviews indicates that even when he described the work of writers whose "philosophy" he opposed, such as Swinburne or Ernest Dowson, he amply appreciated their "beauty," and he never used "morality" as grounds for facile condemnation of his contemporaries. Perhaps even more significant evidence of his critical integrity is his willingness to take exception in print with the theory and practice of his mentors and friends, Coventry Patmore and Alice Meynell. Unlike many writers involved with the Catholic press at the time, Thompson revealed little religious bias in his literary reviews. He praised the founder of Methodism and demolished a "proof" that Shakespeare was Catholic.[88]

Despite this receptivity to art whose ideas opposed his own, however, Thompson implied that the critic's role was a public trust comparable to the poet's, for his job was to generate appreciation for beauty. In "A Lengthy Essay on Poetry," a 1902 review of an *Introduction to Poetry*, he suggested both the overriding purpose and the preferred methods of criticism. Though poetry could not be "taught," love of beauty could be conveyed by criticism—criticism which might more properly be called "appreciation": "The appreciative critic communicates to others his own enjoyment, and as far as possible his own perceptions, of poetry. With this may be combined a certain amount, but not too much, of exposition concerning the formulae and mechanism of verse and poetic style." The aim of criticism is to "stir the slumbering love of poetry."[89] Thompson's own critical practice fit this description particularly well, for he suggested the flavor of the work being discussed, frequently through representative quotations, and only occasionally delved into its "complex elements of technique."[90]

Despite his belief that the critic should apreciate beauty even if he did not share the philosophy of a work, Thompson maintained that the critic's job has moral and ethical dimensions: "Call criticism 'the adventures of a soul among masterpieces,' if you will; but let it be clearly understood that the only valuable adventures are those of the man who is qualified to have them, just as for Aristotle the only valuable moral judgment was that of the man who was fitted by nature and training to express a judgment." Criticism is thus neither "the application of authority" nor "merely an expression of personal preferences or prejudices."[91]

Thompson's evaluations of the major nineteenth-century poets are remarkably consistent with judgments made today. Occasionally he provided insight into the value of works relatively unappreciated at the time he wrote, as in his review of an edition of Dorothy Wordsworth's journals: "We have the finest sympathetic appreciations of nature ever written by any woman, appreciations . . . self-evolved and nursed in the solitude of a soul that deliberately resolved to shut out certain of the joys of life. Sometimes, in reading Dorothy Wordsworth's journals, we seem to hear the cry of an imprisoned spirit."[92] Elsewhere he vividly encapsulates the flavor of a familiar writer, as in a rollicking imaginary account of Walter Savage Landor describing an adventure in Tibet.[93] In sum, his reviews of Romantic and Victorian writers survey the period from the viewpoint of a lively critical intelligence that expresses its judgments with great flair and occasionally delicious touches of wit.

Thompson is perhaps at his critical best when reviewing the works of the seventeenth-century Metaphysical poets. The obvious affinities between their works and his own in 1910 inspired an editor of his essays to formulate a fanciful image: "Truly it seems as if Francis Thompson must have hidden behind Heaven's big front door when Crashaw and Herrick and he were appointed to go dancing out through life, and have played hide-and-go-seek so successfully with the angels that it took them three centuries to catch him."[94] His observations on seventeenth-century writers sparkle with wit and imagery. He judges John Bunyan a bit short on imagination, "a sound trotter, but no Pegasus." Samuel Butler, wanting "a larger portion of good-humour," "is like a hanging judge who is witty at the expense of the prisoner."[95]

Among the seventeenth-century poets Crashaw evoked Thompson's warmest praise. Extended quotation from his observations on Crashaw fittingly conclude a brief survey of Thompson's criticism, primarily because they so aptly describe his own verse. He praises Crashaw's diction—"it thrills and surprises"—as well as his range and variety—

"the triumphant ardour of the longer poems . . . is memorable. And now and again are unexpected turns of the fondest sweetness, like a child's caress." Crashaw "burns and soars, he flames and glances with colour like a humming-bird. His music is exquisite and original as his substance and diction." "Not an impeccable artist," he is nonetheless "a fine artist." Despite his flaws, he offers something rare and rich:

Crashaw . . . is a literary luxury, caviare to the general. To enjoy him needs sympathy and a love of poetry for its own sake. One must be able to appreciate extreme research of language, a lavish and loving richness. One must enjoy the incessant play of a nimble and lightning-like fancy without confounding it with affectation. The man who is wholly enamoured of "simplicity," meaning thereby direct and restrained expression, will recoil from Crashaw. Yet Crashaw is truly simple in spirit: his opulent turns of fancy have the ardent sincerity of a child; his faults of taste come from ardour overshooting its mark, not from ingenuity falling short of it.[96]

Describing Crashaw in 1904, Thompson provided posterity with judgments surely applicable to his own verse, little of which had been published since 1897. It seems fitting that the prose-poet who invented such dramatic and memorable images to characterize other writers—who near the start of his career as an essayist had described Shelley in terms so often applicable to himself—should have penned evaluations that those of us who lack his eloquence can appropriate as tribute to him.

In an essay on Cowley, another of his seventeenth-century favorites, Thompson observed that "in a sense every writer is his own biographer. Just as character—or the want of it—appears in the face, so a man's nature, whether complex or simple, may be inferred from his writings."[97] His book reviews delineate features too rarely hinted by his biographers—wit, urbanity, erudition, geniality, irony, whimsy, analytical power, and most of all an awareness of the world about him often obscured by reports of his trivial self-absorption and unworldliness.

About a year before he died, when his stamina and concentration were sapped increasingly by laudanum and physical deterioration, Thompson projected a collection of his prose. A notebook entry announces his plan and names works to include—some reviews, "*Moestitiae Encomium*," "Modern Men: The Devil," and "Paganism Old and

New." He anticipates some degree of failure: "And so get ready a book for C[onstable]'s refusal. If refused try others." He scolds himself for not having kept copies of back articles. He agonizes over how to track down missing work. He pities himself at the same time as he tries to formulate practical plans. He views the project as something to give him focus, a stay against his accelerating submission to addiction: "Here is work to train your disused muscles."

But a larger purpose also goads him: "On every side, in every way, failure threatens. Yet try, ere the night close utterly in and my prose be lost to posterity after a lifetime of toil not less than set De Quincey at the front of English prose. Pull yourself together at this last, and try it."[98] He did try—he copied selections from his prose into a thick notebook and listed titles of other works. According to Wilfrid Meynell he got as far as "formally correcting . . . for the Press."[99] But like so many other projects in his last few years, the collection of his prose never materialized in his lifetime.

Chapter Six
Conclusion

Because so much of his work has remained unknown, Thompson's literary achievement has not previously been adequately assessed. His prose has not been studied as a body, either for its literary merit or for the insights his reviews offer into the achievement of other writers. Since his death, his poetry has largely appealed to readers for its religious message—as indicated by studies with such titles as *The Catholicity of Francis Thompson* and *Guidance from Francis Thompson in Matters of Faith*—or for the poignant life story detected behind the works—an appeal illustrated by two published dramatizations of his life.[1]

But aside from its religious and biographical interest, his poetry deserves closer scrutiny for its artistry. Most evaluations by his contemporaries, colored to some extent by reviewers' religious affiliations and curiosity about the poet's life, tended to assess the poems in extreme terms, relishing or despising the hyperbolic style of his earliest verse and measuring later publication in terms of expectations created by the first collection.

Reviews tended to assess only the poetry of overstatement, of highly wrought language and mystical dimensions, of a "welter of wonderful words" "wildly abandoned to . . . rapture." Reviewers noted that Thompson's talent and his flaws grew from the same root: his work was "a large utterance—large in bulk, in speed, in a lavish disregard of economy, and yet . . . great and sincere." Arthur Symons praised the poetry in language that characterizes Thompson's talent as impressive but freakish: "The genius of Francis Thompson was Oriental, exuberant in colour, woven into elaborate patterns, and went draped in old silk robes, that had survived many dynasties. The spectacle of him was an enchantment; he passed like a wild vagabond of the mind, dazzling our sight."[2]

Virtually all the contemporary notices focused on the extravagant and easily overstated aspects of his style, and Thompson seems to have regarded himself primarily as the poet of what he called "fireworks."

On the basis of this single side of his poetry, Thompson ranked it
" 'greater' than any work by a new poet which has appeared *since Rossetti*" (though he characteristically hastened to except Alice Meynell).[3]

But the fireworks of "The Hound of Heaven," "Ode to the Setting
Sun," and "A Corymbus for Autumn" distinguish only some of his
work. The religious poet of *"Ex Ore Infantium"* ("Little Jesus"), "The
Kingdom of God," and *"Desiderium Indesideratum"* and the poet of
childhood and nature found in "To Monica: After Nine Years," "To
Stars," "All Flesh," and "Genesis," speak in forcefully quiet, simple
tones, as does the love poet in the later sonnets. Moreover, beneath
both the fireworks and the apparent simplicity, Thompson the craftsman is often experimenting with technical devices and playing against
traditional themes and patterns.

Thompson's literary reputation has fluctuated dramatically since his
death—among Catholic readers rising higher, perhaps, than he mer-
its, but among others falling considerably lower than he deserves.
"The Hound of Heaven" is universally acknowledged as one of the
finest odes in the language. But his florid style in other works famous
in his own day has clearly put off modern readers weaned on T. S.
Eliot. Yet a modern Thompson exists in less well known, and sometimes unavailable, verse. His irony and wit, his evocative understatement, concentrated focus, and quiet idiom await proper appreciation.
Even though Thompson's best work often reveals glaring flaws—gro-
tesque diction, ugly slant rhymes, intrusive decoration, distracting
metaphorical tangents—everywhere his poetry reveals a remarkable
gift of imagery which enriches even slight verse.

Publication of his little-known works and more judicious analysis
of familiar pieces should revise prevailing critical views of Thompson,
who once cautioned, "It is an ill thing to approach a minor writer
with inflamed expectations."[4] The genuine artistry and the diversity
of his total poetic corpus suggest that in Thompson's case, it may be
equally distorting to expect only a minor writer.

Notes and References

Chapter One

1. *The Letters of Francis Thompson*, ed. John E. Walsh (New York: Hawthorn, 1969), 247.

2. Coventry Patmore's praise is cited by Everard Meynell, *The Life of Francis Thompson* (New York: Charles Scribner's Sons, 1913), 191; Viola Meynell offers the consensus view that "in company [he] was mostly silent or repetitive or irrelevant, and never effectual"; *Francis Thompson and Wilfrid Meynell: A Memoir* (New York: Dutton, 1953), 86.

3. E. Meynell, *Life*, 7.

4. *Letters*, 247.

5. Though Everard Meynell and biographers who followed him give December 16 as the birthdate, the later date is supported by Thompson's baptismal record, his registration at Owens Medical College, and the stone tablet placed on his birthplace in 1910.

6. E. Meynell, *Life*, 1.

7. A boyhood friend recalled Thompson's desire for a colorful cassock rather than the standard black; in E. Byrne's "Boyhood Days in Ashton: Francis Thompson," *Ashton Reporter*, December 1930; quoted in John E. Walsh, *Strange Harp, Strange Symphony: The Life of Francis Thompson* (New York: Hawthorn, 1967), 8–9. Quotation given in J. C. Reid, *Francis Thompson: Man and Poet* (London: Routledge & Kegan Paul, 1959), 13.

8. See, e.g., accounts in Walsh, *Strange Harp*, 8–10.

9. His sister Mary was born in 1861, Margaret in 1864. Another sister, Helen Mary, was born in 1862 but died in 1864. The Thompsons also had a son, born before Francis, who lived only one day.

10. Thompson's comment appears in a notebook now in the Thompson Collection at Boston College; his sisters' chiding was recalled by Mary in conversation. Both remarks are cited in Walsh, *Strange Harp*, 8.

11. First cited in E. Meynell, *Life*, 8; Thompson's recollections appear in a manuscript now at Boston College, cited in Walsh, *Strange Harp*, 12.

12. See E. Meynell, *Life*, 26n; Pierre Danchin, *Francis Thompson: La vie et l'oeuvre d'un poète* (Paris: Nizet, 1959), 37 n. 46; John Thomson, *Francis Thompson: Poet and Mystic*, rev. ed. (London: Simpkin, Marshall, Hamilton, Kent, 1923), 27.

13. Wilfrid S. Blunt, *My Diaries* (New York: Knopf, 1932), 594.

14. Recollections in *Ushaw Magazine*, March 1908; cited in Walsh, *Strange Harp*, 15.

15. E. Meynell, *Life*, 32. Francis himself probably realized that he was unsuited for the priesthood and may not have been disappointed to renounce his earlier intentions; see the discussion offered in Walsh, *Strange Harp*, 17–18. Myrtle Pihlman Pope asserts that nowhere do the poet's words confirm that he wanted to be a priest ("A Critical Bibliography of Works by and about Francis Thompson," *Bulletin of the New York Public Library* 63 (1959): 45).

16. *Youthful Verses by Francis Thompson*, ed. Harold Halewood (Preston: privately printed, 1928).

17. Blunt, *Diaries*, 594.

18. Mary emphasized her father's kindness in a letter to Wilfrid Meynell; cited in Walsh, *Strange Harp*, 35–36; Thompson expressed these sentiments to Blunt, reported in his *Diaries*, 594.

19. E. Meynell, *Life*, 60.

20. Notebook entry cited by Reid, *Thompson*, 21.

21. Letter from Edward Healy Thompson to Wilfrid Meynell, cited in Walsh, *Strange Harp*, 22.

22. *Academy*, 29 April 1899; in *The Real Robert Louis Stevenson and Other Critical Essays by Francis Thompson*, ed. Terence L. Connolly (New York: University Publishers, 1959), 111; hereafter cited in the notes and text as *RRLS*.

23. E. Meynell, *Life*, 48.

24. De Quincey set out with "a favourite English poet in one pocket, and an odd volume, containing about one-half of Canter's *Euripides*, in the other"; Thompson carried Blake and Aeschylus.

25. E. Meynell first recorded the story of illness, no doubt following Wilfrid Meynell's suggestion. Wilfrid's younger son Francis (the poet's godson and namesake) later hypothesized that his father had conceived this theory as "a benevolent invention"; see Walsh, *Strange Harp*, 22. Reid (*Thompson*, 21) identifies the illness as "lung fever, the first signs of . . . tuberculosis." One biographer suggests that Thompson suffered a nervous breakdown before leaving home, but offers no evidence for the supposition; see John Thomson, *Francis Thompson*, 35.

26. Notebook entry cited in Walsh, *Strange Harp*, 32–33. Thompson used the image of the toy box in his "Essay on Shelley."

27. Mary Thompson recalled that so many dissection fees finally prompted her father to remark "what a number of corpses he was cutting up"; her letter to Wilfrid Meynell is cited in Walsh, *Strange Harp*, 35.

28. See Walsh, *Strange Harp*, 34 and notes.

29. Thompson described his plans for the volume in a letter from the fall of 1897 (*Letters*, 196–98).

30. *Letters*, 210.

31. "In Darkest England," in *Francis Thompson: Poems and Essays*, 3 vols. in 1, ed. Wilfrid Meynell (Westminster, Md: Newman, 1947), 3:52–53; hereafter cited in the notes and text as *Poems*.

32. E. Meynell, *Life*, 72.
33. Ibid., 70.
34. Walsh, *Strange Harp*, 42–43.
35. *Letters*, 23.
36. Walsh discusses the works associated with this girl, including "Nightmare of the Witch-Babies" and "Sad Semele," in *Strange Harp*, 52–54, 56–60.
37. See Walsh, *Strange Harp*, 79.
38. "Nature's Immortality," *Merry England*, February 1890; quoted in Walsh, *Strange Harp*, 92. Meynell deleted this passage when he published the essay in *Poems*.
39. These and other pseudonyms were used by Thompson and both Meynells.
40. *Letters*, 37. With her assurance, accomplishments, studied charm, and remote loveliness, Alice Meynell entranced many others besides Thompson, most notably Conventry Patmore, who said that he and Thompson shared the bond of mutual, frustrated adoration of her.
41. As examples of Thompson's resistance to criticism of his work and of his acceptance of Alice Meynell's authority, see *Letters*, 48–49, 57–59, 100.
42. Notebook entry cited in *Strange Harp*, 7, and in slightly different form in E. Meynell, *Life*, 12.
43. "The Fourth Order of Humanity," *Poems*, 3:69–70.
44. He once signed a letter, "Ahi! soavissima Madonna Alice, avete pieta di me!" (Oh! sweetest Lady Alice, have pity on me!); *Letters*, 86.
45. Ibid.
46. E. Meynell, *Life*, 230.
47. Thompson recorded the range of their conversations in his notebook: "Nonsense verses . . . Browning . . . seeing the invisible . . . Swedenborg mad . . . Intense flame of life in Raphael's women . . . Dreams . . . Sun vibrates . . . future of Europe—Virginity of soul in fallen woman . . . X-rays. Science will have to be stopped. . . ." The fuller listing from which these topics have been excerpted appears in Walsh, *Strange Harp*, 146.
48. Patmore wrote to Thompson: "If, at any time, you find yourself seriously ill, and do not find the attendance, food, &c., sufficiently good, tell me and I will go to Pantasaph to take care of you for any time you might find me useful." Cited in E. Meynell, *Life*, 233.
49. See *Strange Harp*, 165ff., for Walsh's revisionist discussion of Thompson's continued pursuit of Katie King.
50. Wilfred Whitten's remarks recorded in E. Meynell, *Life*, 253.
51. Reviews quoted by Reid, *Thompson*, 159. Not all reviews were so harsh, and in December 1897 the *Morning Post* named *New Poems* the best volume of poetry published that year; see *Letters*, 194–95.
52. See Walsh, *Strange Harp*, 178–79.

53. Loose notebook page, quoted in Walsh, *Strange Harp*, 179–80, and more fully in Danchin, *Thompson*, 121–22 n. 54.

54. E. Meynell, *Life*, 242–43.

55. See *Letters*, 93, 201.

56. E. Meynell, *Life*, 253.

57. When the staff of the *Athenaeum* began to pretend they needed his copy a day earlier than they actually did, Thompson realized the reason for the subterfuge and exhorted himself in a notebook: "Remember the new *Athenaeum* dodge testifies against you" (V. Meynell, *Memoir*, 123).

58. E. Meynell, *Life*, 319–20.

59. V. Meynell, *Memoir*, 158.

60. E. Meynell, *Life*, 132.

Chapter Two

1. Paul van Kuykendall Thomson, *Francis Thompson: A Critical Biography* (New York: Nelson, 1961), 94.

2. "Ode to the Setting Sun" appeared in revised form in *New Poems* (1897). It may have been omitted from *Poems* because Wilfrid Meynell thought "violence of diction" marred it, or because readers had protested against its paganism; see Reid, *Thompson*, 93, and *Letters*, 35.

3. In "Ode to the Setting Sun" Thompson's images of beauty breaking forth in a red glow from something dying strikingly resemble Gerard Manley Hopkins's image of ashes gashing themselves "gold vermillion" to suggest the implicit glory of the Crucifixion in "God's Grandeur," written in 1877 but unpublished until 1918. Although no connection has been demonstrated, Thompson may have become acquainted with Hopkins's work through his friendship with Coventry Patmore, who had read Hopkins's poetry in manuscript in 1884. See *Further Letters of Gerard Manley Hopkins*, ed. C. C. Abbott, 2d ed. (London: Oxford, 1956), 352–54.

4. *Letters*, 98.

5. Reid, *Thompson*, 82, 210.

6. Thompson's argument that Nature has established proper limits for everything sounds remarkably like Pope's assertion that "Nature to all things fixed the limits fit" (*An Essay on Criticism*, 1:52). Moreover, Thompson's suggestion that Nature appropriately limited his optical power to gauge the lady's merit ("So high constructing Nature lessons to us all: / Who optics gives accommodate to see / Your countenance large as looks the sun to be, / And distant greatness less than near humanity") echoes rather specifically Pope's optical metaphor in *An Essay on Man* illustrating why man has limited capacities (Epistle 1, ll. 189–200).

7. See *Letters*, 100. Thompson's note in the manuscript of another poem, "The Perfect Woman," indicates that he intended it to follow "*Domus*

Tua." It continues the dwelling metaphor, but in lines technically less successful. See *The Man Has Wings: New Poems and Plays by Francis Thompson,* ed. Terence L. Connolly (Garden City, N.Y.: Hanover House, 1957), 30; hereafter cited in the notes and text as *MHW*.

8. Walsh, *Strange Harp,* 43.

9. Ibid., 11.

10. Thompson's satiric spirit in the poem is suggested by his comments regarding the playful rhyming variations on the Old English line: "The minor versifier has at any rate the asterisks in 'A Judgment in Heaven' which he can catch on to. There he can have the latest device in poetry, the whole apparatus procurable at my printer's" (*Letters,* 111).

11. P. Thomson, *Thompson,* 103.

12. Besides the similar situation, details in Byron's poem may echo in "A Judgment in Heaven." Byron's description of angels playing with stars may, for example, have influenced Thompson's angels who "Looked up from disport . . . as they pelted each other with handfuls of stars."

13. Thompson ranked Browning very high among contemporary poets and was gratified when in 1889 Browning thanked Meynell generously for sending him copies of Thompson's "remarkable" poems. Browning's letter may indicate greater interest in the dramatic situation of Thompson's striving to overcome his addiction than in the poetry itself: "It is altogether extraordinary that a young man so naturally gifted should need incitement to do justice to his own conspicuous ability by endeavouring to emerge from so uncongenial a course of life as that which you describe. . . . Pray assure him, if he cares to know it, that I have a confident expectation of his success, if he will but extricate himself—as by a strenuous effort he may—from all that must now embarrass him terribly." Cited in Reid, *Thompson,* 63.

14. P. Thomson, *Thompson,* 96.

15. "Epipsychidion," ll. 273–74; and *Prometheus Unbound,* 4:73–76. On Thompson's use of sources, see Reid, *Thompson,* 82–84, and Walsh, *Strange Harp,* 92–100.

16. Cited in Walsh, *Strange Harp,* 100.

17. *Letters,* 115.

18. Ibid., 77.

19. This image also appears in Thompson's prose "A Threnody of Birth," in *RRLS,* 296.

20. Mary's role here may echo the medieval tradition that in bearing the innocent flesh of Christ, she was weaving a perfect cloth without seam.

21. The poem first appeared in the June 1891 *Merry England.*

22. Wilfrid Meynell prints these excerpts from reviews in his edition of *Selected Poems of Francis Thompson* (London: Methuen, Burns & Oates, 1910), 137, 136, 135.

23. *Letters,* 61–62.

24. Ibid., 128. At about the same time John Lane published the work, Wilfrid Meynell had a limited number of copies privately printed as *Songs Wing-to-Wing*.

25. *Letters*, 126.

Chapter Three

1. *Letters*, 177. Thompson's chosen title for the 1897 volume may suggest his sense of new beginning, and Reid (*Thompson*, 140) observes, the titles he considered but rejected "indicate the importance he attached to the different note sounded in the book—*Songs of the Inner Life, Night Before Light,* and *The Dawn Before the Day-Star.*"

2. *Letters*, 156. *New Poems* included forty-five poems never before published, eight that had previously appeared in *Merry England,* and one that had been published in the *Athenaeum*.

3. See P. Thomson, *Thompson*, 130–31.

4. *Letters*, 149.

5. Ibid.

6. Cited in Reid, *Thompson*, 158.

7. Penciled draft in Boston College notebook; cited in *Letters*, 92.

8. *Letters*, 116.

9. Walsh, *Strange Harp*, 54.

10. A stiff, petulant letter that Thompson wrote to Alice Meynell in September 1892 illustrates his alienation from someone who failed to keep an appointment with him, as well as his exaggerated constraint about speaking openly on such matters. See *Letters*, 84–86.

11. E. Meynell, *Life*, 230–31.

12. From "Mr. Meredith as Poet," *Academy*, 3 October 1903; in *RRLS*, 131. It has been suggested that Thompson "discovered Meredith as a poet" during an overnight visit he and Alice Meynell made to the novelist's home at Box Hill in late June 1896, after he had already completed the proofs for *New Poems* (P. Thomson, *Thompson*, 146). But Thompson quoted from Meredith's verse in an undated letter which Walsh assigns to 15 July 1892, and which certainly antedates 1896 (*Letters*, 76). Thompson linked Meredith and Browning as poets of "a peculiar quality" unparalleled in English poetry (*RRLS*, 126). He discussed *James Lee's Wife* in "Browning Re-considered," *Academy*, 25 October 1902; in *Literary Criticism by Francis Thompson*, ed. Terence L. Connolly (New York: Dutton, 1948), 155–56.

13. Walsh, *Strange Harp*, 54; see also *Letters*, 150–51.

14. *Letters*, 150.

15. *Letters*, 185–86; Walsh offers this perceptive interpretation of the letter. P. Thomson (*Thompson*, 112–13), in contrast, suggests that Thompson felt "some continuing personal conflict" over the content of the poems.

16. Thompson explained the autobiographical significance of *Ultima* by describing his renunciation of Alice Meynell, whom he "loved more than my love of her family"; cited in P. Thomson, *Thompson*, 112. The adoration of the *Ultima* speaker may be seen, for example, in a letter Thompson wrote Alice Meynell in September 1892, declaring "I am unhappy when I am out of your sight; and would pass every hour, if I could, in your exquisite presence, only to feel the effluence of your spirit in contact with mine" (*Letters*, 86).

17. These lines may refer to the Meynells' distress, precipitating their visit to Pantasaph, over reports that Thompson remained "the best part of the day" in bed and may have reverted to drug consumption. See E. Meynell, *Life*, 143–44, and P. Thomson, *Thompson*, 110–11.

18. Walsh, *Strange Harp*, 143. In a letter written in August 1892 Thompson explained in detail that he rejected Patmore's views: "The permanence of carnal delight in the Heavenly union would to me make it un-heavenly. Even here on earth, my own instinct as to the typical union . . . would be a union like that of the Virgin and St. Joseph." He concluded that "If mystic theology is ever to form a part of my life, it must be what God shall teach me, not Coventry Patmore, nor another" (*Letters*, 80, 82). Rossetti may also have influenced Thompson's later association of carnal and spiritual love.

19. *Letters*, 112–13. Patmore reviewed *Poems* in the *Fortnightly Review*, January 1894.

20. "A Poet's Religion," in *Literary Criticisms*, 211. Walsh points up the application to Thompson's view of his own work in *Strange Harp*, 145.

21. See P. Thomson, *Thompson*, 122–25. For Thompson's discussion of meter, see "Style and the 'Edinburgh Review,' " *Academy*, 18 November 1899; in *RRLS*, 234; "Poetry" and "Dante's Metrics," in *The Lost Poems of Francis Thompson*, ed. Myrtle Pihlman Pope (Ann Arbor: University Microfilms, 1966), 14–23; hereafter cited in the notes and text as *LP*.

22. This association is reinforced by Shelleyan vocabulary such as "skiey" and "lovelily," but such diction permeates Thompson's works.

23. See *Letters*, 28. Though in that letter Thompson had declared of Coleridge, "I early recognised that to make him a model was like trying to run up a window-pane, or to make clotted cream out of moonlight, or to pack jelly-fish in hampers," an early commentator, Sir Arthur Quiller-Couch, associated "The Mistress of Vision" with "Kubla Khan"; see notice in the *Daily News*, cited in *Selected Poems*, 140.

24. Reid (*Thompson*, 105) regards the passage rhyming "Himalay" and "Cathay" as an incongruous echo of Rudyard Kipling's "Mandalay."

25. *Letters*, 131; and notebook entry cited in Reid, *Thompson*, 115.

26. The essay fragment appears in *RRLS*, 319–24. For further discussion of Thompson's theory of symbolism, see P. Thomson, *Thompson*, 138–39.

27. *Letters*, 132.

28. Reid (*Thompson*, 105) detects specific echoes of Wordsworth's "Tintern Abbey." *Sight and Insight* as a whole is heavily imbued with ideas characteristic of Romantic literature.

29. Thompson wrote that in addition to the liturgical office he had drawn material from "the Canticle," "heathen mythology," and "a hymn of St. Nerses the Armenian" (*Letters*, 109–10). Several months later Thompson commented that "*Assumpta Maria*" did not "come to much" (Ibid., 113).

30. Arthur Symons complained (*Athenaeum*, 3 February 1894), "If Crashaw, Shelley, Donne, Marvell, Patmore and some other poets had not existed, Francis Thompson would be a poet of remarkable novelty . . . his work, with all its splendours, has the impress of no individuality; it is a splendour of rags and patches"; cited in *Letters*, 115. Thompson in turn judged Symons "the only critic of mine I think downright unfair" (Ibid., 130). Some twentieth-century critics (e.g., Reid, *Thompson*, 104–5) seem particularly critical of Thompson's borrowings and echoes, but Walsh (*Strange Harp*, 93–100, e.g.) demonstrates how Thompson can turn an echo or allusion to remarkably fresh effect. Thompson discussed the unavoidability and the merit of literary echoes in "Literary Coincidence," *Merry England*, April 1889; in *Literary Criticisms*, 451–56.

31. See George Ferguson, *Signs and Symbols in Christian Art* (New York: Oxford University Press, 1961), 18; and Beryl Rowland, *Birds with Human Souls: A Guide to Bird Symbolism* (Knoxville: University of Tennessee Press, 1978), 58–63.

32. Rowland, *Birds*, 62–63.

33. *Letters*, 134.

34. See P. Thomson, *Thompson*, 122.

35. *Letters*, 138. In 1892 Thompson had argued against revising previously published poetry. Although he was speaking about all poetry, which "to a certain degree . . . is a portrait," he referred specifically to work by Alice Meynell which he considered "*in excelsis*" a "portrait of [her] youthful self" (Ibid., 78).

36. Ibid., 128–29.

37. P. Thomson, *Thompson*, 133.

38. Reid, *Thompson*, 139, 150.

39. *Letters*, 120.

40. Ibid., 65–66. Neither essay was published until after Thompson died.

41. Thompson's comments have led Walsh to connect "An Anthem of Earth" with Shakespeare's *Timon of Athens*, on which Thompson had begun preparing a commentary in the spring preceding composition of the poem; see *Strange Harp*, 148–49. Thompson's 1893 description of a passage from *Timon* as "a magnificent ode in miniature" (*RRLS*, 165) supports the suggestion.

42. See, e.g., Reid, *Thompson,* 150.

43. Referring to the phrase "Pontifical Death," which appears in "An Anthem of Earth" (and also in the prose "Out of the House of Bondage") G. K. Chesterton discussed Thompson's fecund talent for implying multiple connotations: "he says that the abyss between the known and the unknown is bridged by 'Pontifical death.' There are about ten historical and theological puns in that one word. That a priest means a pontiff, that a pontiff means a bridge-maker, that death is certainly a bridge, that death may turn out after all to be a reconciling priest, that at least priest and bridges both attest to the fact that one thing can get separated from another thing—these ideas, and twenty more, are all tacitly concentrated in the word 'Pontifical' "; notice in the *Illustrated London News,* cited in *Selected Poems,* 141.

44. "Shelley," *Poems,* 3:37. See W. G. Wilson, "Francis Thompson's Outlook on Science," *Contemporary Review* 192 (1957):263–66.

45. *Letters,* 30, 40, 34.

46. Ibid., 132. Thompson penned several verse memorials after Patmore's death; see *MHW,* 61–63.

47. *Letters,* 247.

48. Manuscript critique of Coventry Patmore's odes, in *RRLS,* 334–38.

49. Thompson's footnote in *New Poems* (182) records that "The first two stanzas are from a French original—I have forgotten what."

50. The poem is probably one of two that Thompson affectionately referred to as "bantlings in verse" (*Letters,* 96). It seems to have been completed by April 1893, and Thompson suggested that if he had kept the manuscript for the 1893 *Poems* longer, he would have included the lyric in the section of poems on children (Ibid., 103).

51. *Letters,* 185–86. "A Colourist in Poetry," *Academy,* 15 July 1899; in *RRLS,* 115.

52. Reid, *Thompson,* 139. His critics have differed with Thompson and with each other on the number of neologisms and archaisms in *New Poems.* According to Reid, Frederick B. Tolles counts 183 obsolete, archaic, and rare words in Thompson's published corpus, with nearly half, eighty-eight, in *New Poems.* Of the 134 coinages he finds in Thompson, seventy-six appear in this last volume. But word counting proves to be no simple matter. Paul Thomson (*Thompson,* 153), in contrast, maintains that a check of the *Oxford English Dictionary* reveals that of the 134 word coinages identified by G. A. Beacock, only seven deserve the label; Thompson otherwise merely uses existing terms in innovative ways. See Beacock, *Francis Thompson* (Marburg: R. Noske, 1912), 79–86.

53. Walsh, *Strange Harp,* 140, 142.

54. *Letters,* 191–92.

55. Ibid., 194–95.

56. Ibid., 156.

57. Ibid., 177.
58. Walsh, *Strange Harp*, 153.

Chapter Four

1. The important additions to the Thompson canon are the collections edited by Wilfrid Meynell in 1913, Connolly in 1957, and Pope in 1966. Throughout this chapter these sources are identified by abbreviations in parentheses. Poems for which no such identification appears exist in manuscripts in the Thompson Collection of Boston College. Walsh's *Strange Harp* has printed a substantial number of works, though some only in fragments. I am at present preparing a complete critical edition of Francis Thompson's poetry, including manuscript material never before published.

2. From "Ode to the English Martyrs" Meynell deleted forty-seven lines which prophesy doom for a debased world; see Walsh, *Strange Harp*, 203.

3. "Excursions in Criticism," *Academy*, 23 October 1897; in *Literary Criticisms*, 245. Thompson also criticized poets who "diluted their inspired work with floods of absolute or comparative mediocrity," "Christina Rossetti," *Athenaeum*, 2 April 1904; in *RRLS*, 143.

4. For a discussion of the nature of these journals, see Pope, "A Critical Bibliography," 62 (1958):571–75.

5. On the Meynells' advice he withdrew *"Domus Tua"* from the sequence *Love in Dian's Lap*, published in *Poems*. See *Letters*, 100.

6. *Letters*, 198.

7. See Walsh, *Strange Harp*, 166; and *Letters*, 206.

8. *Letters*, 206.

9. "The Train" appears in *MHW*, 76; the satire on the Philistines is "The Larger Hope," ibid., 82–83. Several bits of satire on figures from the Boer War exist in unpublished manuscripts.

10. See, for example, "The Bird" and "Lover's Progress" in *LP*, 47, 49.

11. See a longer version of the cricket verses in Everard Meynell, "The Notebooks of Francis Thompson," *Dublin Review*, January 1917, 109–22.

12. Printed in Walsh, *Strange Harp*, 104.

13. *Letters*, 42.

14. Ibid., 34.

15. Revealed by Everard Meynell's notebook, cited in Walsh, *Strange Harp*, 69. Terence Connolly also chose not to publish the poem, which exists in a Thompson notebook at Boston College. Walsh published it in *Strange Harp*, 57–60.

16. Printed in Walsh, *Strange Harp*, 47–48.

17. See discussion of this prose work in chapter 5.

18. Printed in Walsh, *Stange Harp*, 50.

19. Most of this poem is printed in Walsh, *Strange Harp*, 129–31.

20. In the manuscript notebook Thompson first wrote a prose draft of the poem; quoted in Walsh, *Strange Harp*, 273.

21. Under the title "Of My Friend" Meynell published two of the eighteen stanzas (*Poems*, 2:211). For Thompson's criticism of this poem, see *Letters*, 212.

22. Printed in Walsh, *Strange Harp*, 156.

23. "Out of the House of Bondage," in *RRLS*, 305, 307.

24. These lines may literally indicate that Katie was writing to him.

25. In his biography of Thompson, Pierre Danchin prints the full fourteen lines as edited by Francis Meynell, Wilfrid's younger son and Thompson's godson. Francis's choices from the variant readings left unresolved in the rough draft obscure the sonnet rhyme scheme that Connolly's edition of the ten lines observes. See Danchin, *Thompson*, 240.

26. See Walsh, *Strange Harp*, 179, 275–76 n.4.

27. *Letters*, 211–12.

28. The four poems are printed in full in Walsh, *Strange Harp*, 28–30.

29. The poem could conceivably apply to Maggie Brien, who, as *A Narrow Vessel* makes plain, inspired poetry that she could not understand or adequately value. Moreover, Thompson's analysis of her nature, though it gave birth to his poetic sequence, also effectively destroyed their relationship as lovers. The poet's extreme sympathy for the Semele figure, however, makes the association with the girl of the streets more likely.

30. Printed in Walsh, *Strange Harp*, 258–59.

31. *Letters*, 206–7.

32. The volume title, description of the section on children, motto, and dedicatory poem all appear in a notebook in the Boston College collection.

33. For Thompson's appreciation of Whitman, see, e.g., "American Culture," *Academy*, 20 October 1906; in *Literary Criticisms*, 323.

34. In manuscript this poem was entitled by Thompson "In No Strange Land." Above that title Wilfrid Meynell added the name by which it is more familiarly known.

35. *Letters*, 47.

36. Ibid. "John Henry Newman" was not reprinted; Walsh quotes it in *Strange Harp*, 263 n. 8.

37. See Walsh, *Strange Harp*, 169.

38. A notice of Queen Victoria's death in 1901 also seems to have been uncommissioned. The labored character of "Victoria Regina, In Memoriam" (*MHW*, 67–69) is observable in its self-conscious reference to Thompson's "customed style" of beginning poems.

39. *Letters*, 216.

40. Ibid., 259.

41. Ibid., 257. Before sending the ode to the journal, Meynell excised forty-seven lines which berate the modern age.

Chapter Five

1. Foreword, *Literary Criticisms*, vii.

2. Eleven of these signed reviews appeared in 1897–1898, perhaps bearing Thompson's name because he hoped to call Mrs. King's attention to his industry and solvency. For a description of the journals to which Thompson contributed regularly, see Pope, "Critical Bibliography," 62 (1958):571–75.

3. Wilfrid Meynell verified Thompson's authorship of these articles. Attributions of Thompson's anonymous work in other journals were based on his correspondence, telegrams he received that acknowledged receipt of his manuscripts, files of the journals, and passages in his poetry that closely parallel the phrasing of the prose articles.

4. Reid, *Thompson*, 189–90.

5. Thompson's letters from 1905 and 1906 frequently lament that he failed to deliver pages and collect his money before Everard's bookshop closed, or promise to bring an installment the following day. See, for example, *Letters*, 236, 238–42.

6. "The Essay: Ancient and Modern," *Academy*, 20 June 1903; in *RRLS*, 286.

7. *RRLS*, 289.

8. *Letters*, 23.

9. See *Letters*, 39; and Walsh, *Strange Harp*, 69.

10. "Paganism Old and New," in *Poems*, 3:39, 51; hereafter page references cited in the text.

11. Just four years after Thompson used the phrase "New Paganism" to mean an essentially Christian recasting of the myths of antiquity, the phrase had gained currency among the Aesthetes and Decadents to suggest the sensationalism of their art. In August 1892 appeared the first and only issue of the *Pagan Review*, written by William Sharp and designed to promote the "New Paganism." See Holbrook Jackson, *The Eighteen Nineties* (1913; reprint, New York: Capricorn, 1966), 22.

12. Discussing the spirituality of modern love poetry, Thompson quotes from the works of such classical writers as Catullus, Ovid, and Propertius, and from moderns ranging from Chaucer to Rossetti. Although it has been suggested that as Thompson was working on this essay during his comparatively ordered life at McMaster's bootshop, he could have consulted texts for these quotations, Thompson himself indicated to Wilfrid Meynell that he drew from memory the extensive quotations and allusions in this essay; see E. Meynell, *Life*, 89–90.

13. In more impish moods Thompson could treat marriage humor-

ously: "It has been suggested, indeed, that Christ at Cana plainly thought a man could not go through with marriage, except he had much wine" ("Modern Men: The Devil," *RRLS*, 310).

14. *Letters*, 35.

15. "A Lengthy Essay on Poetry," *Academy*, 19 July 1902; in *RRLS*, 278.

16. See Walsh, *Strange Harp*, 103, 259 n. 2.

17. Thompson praises Poe's fiction in a later review, "A Dreamer of Things Impossible," *Academy*, 28 September 1901; in *Literary Criticisms*, 317–22. He quotes Poe's poetry in his earlier prose, e.g., "Stray Thoughts on Shelley," *A Renegade Poet and Other Essays*, ed. Edward J. O'Brien (Boston: Ball, 1910), 127–28; hereafter cited in the text as *RP* with page number.

18. "*Finis Coronat Opus*," in *Poems*, 3:116.

19. For harsh criticisms, sometimes linking the tale to Thompson's own life, see Walsh, *Strange Harp*, 87; Derek Stanford, "Francis Thompson's Prose," *Month*, n.s. 18 (1957): 305; Reid, *Thompson*, 177, 179.

20. The tale's correspondences to the essay include Florentian's inability to love a woman or Nature, his insensitivity to Aster's spiritually charged eyes, and the fickleness of popular appreciation of true poetry.

21. "Poems of Ernest Dowson," manuscript in Boston College collection; printed in *Literary Criticisms*, 560. For Thompson's criticisms of the Art for Art's Sake and Decadent movements, see, e.g., "The Claim of the Artist," *Academy*, 12 October 1901; in *RRLS*, 268–73.

22. "A Colourist in Poetry," *Academy*, 15 July 1899; in *RRLS*, 113. See also similar objections to Art for Art's Sake in "Mr. Swinburne," *Academy*, 23 March 1901, in *RRLS*, 156. It is important to note that Thompson also objected to poetry that was concerned with moral and ethical doctrine at the expense of art. See, e.g., "Christina Rossetti," *Athenaeum*, 2 April 1904; in *RRLS*, 143.

23. Reid, *Thompson*, 179.

24. "*Moestitiae Encomium*," *Poems*, 3:111.

25. *Letters*, 151–52. Many of the contributors to the *Yellow Book* and the *Savoy* published their works with John Lane or with Elkin Matthews, Lane's former partner.

26. See *RP*, 202. Thompson comically satirizes the "new realism" in paintings of biblical scenes in "The Trecentisti up to Dante," a manuscript in Boston College collection; in *RRLS*, 325–30.

27. "Health and Holiness," in *Poems*, 3:276–77.

28. "The Image of God," in *Literary Criticisms*, 492–93. Thompson also acknowledged the burden of one's physical existence. His letters are full of complaints about infirmities.

29. "Poems of Ernest Dowson," *Literary Criticisms*, 560. Thompson also associated emphasis on form with "French reaction," in a review of "Mr. Henley's New Poems," *Weekly Register*, 21 May 1892; in *RRLS*, 117.

30. "Form and Formalism," *Franciscan Annals*, March 1893, in *Poems*, 3:71, 74.

31. Thompson reiterated the importance of individuality, though not in a literary context, in a manuscript entitled "Out of the House of Bondage," in Boston College collection; in *RRLS*, 303–8.

32. "The Way of Imperfection," in *Poems*, 3:97; hereafter page references given in the text.

33. Although his poetic style usually contrasts starkly with Browning's, Thompson's praise of imperfection and mannerisms associates him with the aesthetic theory manifest not only in Browning, but also in Ruskin, Hopkins, and other Victorians.

34. "A Monument of Personality," *Academy*, 29 April 1899; in *RRLS*, 109.

35. "*Anima Simplicitatis*," manuscript in Boston College collection; in *RRLS*, 314; hereafter page references given in the text. Thompson discussed related ideas in a review, "On Obscurity in Verse," *Academy*, 9 March 1901.

36. "Analogies Between God, Nature, Man and the Poet," manuscript in Boston College collection; in *RRLS*, 346. Thompson referred to his unpublished fragment in a letter written to Coventry Patmore in June 1893 (*Letters*, 97). See also his comments on "a type of poetic imagination that beholds the world shot through and through with symbolism and caught in a network of strange relations beyond the plain man's understanding," in "A New Anthology," *Academy*, 13 November 1897; in *RRLS*, 134.

37. Two manuscript fragments, "A Preface and Essay on Symbolism," develop this analogy between poetic symbolism and Nature's symbolizing God; in *RRLS*, 319–24. See also the discussion of the poet's discerning "the real order of things" through his unity with Nature, in "A Poet on Poetry," *Academy*, 10 March 1900; in *RRLS*, 236–37.

38. "Analogies Between God, Nature, Man and the Poet," *RRLS*, 346–47. (In this quotation I have silently expanded Thompson's abbreviations for *imagination*.) In a letter Thompson quoted himself to chastise Coventry Patmore for confusing the terms *fancy* and *imagination* (*Letters*, 97–98). See also his discussion of *fancy* and *imagination* in "A Poet on Poetry," in *RRLS*, 237.

39. *Letters*, 38.

40. Ibid., 31.

41. Wyndham's letter is reprinted in *Poems*, 3:283–85.

42. *Letters*, 36. The poetic intensity of his prose is equally obvious in an essay he never printed, "A Threnody of Birth," probably written in 1890 or 1891, whole passages of which appear almost verbatim in the later poem "An Anthem of Earth" (written 1894). Thompson had sent the essay to the *National Observer*, whose editor William Ernest Henley apparently rejected it (*Letters*, 65). The essay, manuscript at Boston College, is printed in *RRLS*, 295–98.

43. "Shelley," *Dublin Review*, July 1908; printed in *Poems*, 3:18.

Thompson discussed Shelley again in an article published in the *Academy*, 22 May 1897 (*RRLS*, 146–49), and earlier in "Stray Thoughts on Shelley," in the September 1892 *Merry England;* printed in *A Renegade Poet*, 109–28.

44. *Letters*, 38.

45. Ibid., 36.

46. "A Modern Study of Sanctity," *Academy*, 13 August 1898; in *Literary Criticisms*, 450.

47. "Health and Holiness," in *Poems*, 3:260–61.

48. "The Prophet as Poet," *Academy*, 29 January 1898; in *RRLS*, 216–19.

49. "Form and Formalism," in *Poems*, 3:71.

50. "A Renegade Poet on the Poet," *Merry England*, July 1892; in *Poems*, 3:105.

51. This analogy to political revolution illustrates that although Thompson is depicted in biographies and memoirs as a wholly unworldly figure, he often slips into his prose social and political comments that indicate that he was not only aware of the world, but judged it incisively, as illustrated by his wry observation on kings in the "Shelley" essay: "is it not a mere fact . . . that in all European countries, except two, monarchs are a mere survival, the obsolete buttons on the coat-tails of rule, which serve no purpose but to be continually coming off?" (*Poems*, 3:33). Thompson deplored "great minuteness of word selection" in contemporary novelists as well as poets, in "Style and the 'Edinburgh Review,' " *Academy*, 18 November 1899; in *RRLS*, 232. On "words for words' sake" as "a kind of gospel" that had poets of the Nineties searching for words in dictionaries and old books, see Jackson, *The Eighteen Nineties*, 135.

52. In a note intended for inclusion in *New Poems* Thompson said he had curbed his use of neologisms and archaisms and "modified much the excessive loading both of diction and imagery which disfigured my former work" (Reid, *Thompson*, 139).

53. "A Lengthy Essay on Poetry," *Academy*, 19 July 1902; in *RRLS*, 281.

54. "Shelley," *Poems*, 3:6.

55. *Letters*, 192–93.

56. Ibid., 57.

57. Ibid.

58. "The Rough Drafts of Creation," *Academy*, 12 October 1901; in *RRLS*, 275. Unlike many Victorians who could not reconcile scientific and theological views of creation, Thompson harmonized them with this notion that extinct species are "rough drafts" preliminary to creation. In a book review written a decade earlier he had not judged theories of evolution but had demanded that adherents of Darwin support their hypotheses with proof; "A Century of Revolution," *Weekly Register*, 12 April 1890; in *Literary Criticisms*, 484–90.

59. "Health and Holiness," *Poems*, 3:281, 258.

60. "Tennyson Re-considered," *Academy*, 18 October 1902; in *RRLS*, 172.

61. *Letters*, 101–2.

62. "Nature's Immortality," in *Poems*, 3:82.

63. Walsh (*Strange Harp*, 31) says the essay illustrates "the misty, half-unrealized mental landscape in which [Thompson] roamed."

64. "The Fourth Order of Humanity," *Merry England*, December 1891, in *Poems*, 3:67.

65. "Shelley," *Poems*, 3:34. On Thompson's satire, see P. Thomson, *Thompson*, 227–36.

66. "Renegade Poet on the Poet," *Poems*, 3:106–7.

67. "In Darkest England," *Poems*, 3:62.

68. "Catholics in Darkest England," *Merry England*, January 1891; printed in Walsh, *Strange Harp*, 50.

69. *Letters*, 210.

70. Ibid., 197–98.

71. The work was completed by Alice Meynell from a different knowledge of the city (*Letters*, 198).

72. Ibid., 221–22.

73. Ibid., 65–66.

74. "Modern Men: The Devil," manuscript in Boston College collection; in *RRLS*, 309, 313.

75. "Hudibras-Butler," *Academy*, 11 February 1905; in *Literary Criticisms*, 58.

76. *Letters*, 73. Walsh reports that Everard Meynell recorded a note for his *Life:* "W. B. Yeats and the Rhymers' Club. Francis once attended with some scorn" (*Strange Harp*, 264 n. 25).

77. Walsh, *Strange Harp*, 118.

78. The first two of these plays appear in *MHW*. The *Saul* manuscript, in the Boston College collection, remains unpublished. Walsh records (*Strange Harp*, 52) that Thompson wrote a playlet, set in classical Rome, in which a scene evokes his relationship to the unnamed prostitute who befriended him.

79. P. Thomson (*Thompson*, 202) speculates that "Thompson had no contact whatever with the stage. In fact, it seems unlikely that he ever witnessed a professional performance of any contemporary play." But he also observes (235) that an entry in Thompson's Large Commonplace Book describes "melodramatic contemporary actors" with faces like "boiling porridge" that temporarily displayed "ready-prepared emotion" before subsiding again into "ponderous agglutination." As a boy Thompson had participated in amateur theatricals at his church; probably during the period of 1897–1899 he recorded his desire "to try private acting," especially in the Shakespearean roles Hamlet, Shylock, and Richard III, but "the difficulty is to get . . . the

most moderately efficient amateur support" (Walsh, *Strange Harp*, 11, 246–47 n. 11).

80. *Letters*, 215–16. Archer, an early translator and defender of Ibsen, has been called "the father of modern dramatic criticism" in England (Jackson, *The Eighteen Nineties*, 207).

81. Thompson's view of Napoleon expressed in a book review written at about the same time as the play provides a complement to this melodramatic portrayal; see "Napoleon by Flashlights," *Academy*, 8 January 1898; in *RRLS*, 10–14.

82. E. Meynell, *Life*, 337 n. 1.

83. Ibid.

84. "Promise," *Academy*, 16 August 1902; in *RRLS*, 187, 188.

85. See "A Kentucky Poet," *Academy*, 13 September, 1902; "The Poet-Priest of America," *Weekly Register*, 17 August 1895; in *RRLS*, 179–81, 190–93.

86. See essays on the Irish Literary Revival and Yeats in *RRLS*, 194–215.

87. *Letters*, 192.

88. See "Manifest Hard Work," *Academy*, 6 June 1903, and "Was Shakespeare a Catholic?," *Academy*, 17 June 1899; in *RRLS*, 47–51, 226–31.

89. "A Lengthy Essay on Poetry," *Academy*, 19 July 1902; in *RRLS*, 279.

90. When Thompson did focus on a poet's technique, the results were particularly illuminating, as, for example, in his comments on the onomatopoeic effects of diction in a line by Keats, in "The Study of Poetry," *Academy*, 16 March 1901; in *RRLS*, 250.

91. "A New Anthology," *Academy*, 13 November 1897; in *RRLS*, 133–34.

92. "Dorothy Wordsworth," *Academy*, 4 November 1905; in *RRLS*, 52.

93. "Landor and Rose-Water," *Academy*, 18 February 1899; in *Literary Criticisms*, 34–35.

94. *A Renegade Poet*, 18–19.

95. "The Pilgrim's Progress—After Two Centuries," *Academy*, 27 August 1898, and "Hudibras-Butler," *Academy*, 11 February 1905; in *Literary Criticisms*, 50, 60, 61.

96. "Crashaw," *Athenaeum*, 24 September 1904; in *RRLS*, 68–69.

97. "Cowley Redivivus," *Academy*, 1 November 1902; in *RRLS*, 64.

98. Notebook entry dating from late 1906, quoted in Walsh, *Strange Harp*, 206.

99. *Poems*, 3:ii.

Chapter Six

    1. Francis Doogan, *The Catholicity of Francis Thompson* (Melbourne: Australian Catholic Truth Society, n.d.); John A. Hutton, *Guidance from Francis Thompson in Matters of Faith* (London: Hodder & Stoughton, 1926); biographical dramatizations include Felix Doherty, *Song Out of Sorrow* (Boston: Bruce Humphries, 1942); and Jack De Leon, *Francis Thompson* (London: Fortune, 1945).

    2. These notices are all quoted in *Selected Poems*.

    3. *Letters*, 111.

    4. "Minor Poets of the Caroline Period," *Athenaeum*, 5 August 1905; in *RRLS*, 60.

Selected Bibliography

PRIMARY SOURCES

1. Poetry, First Editions

New Poems. London: Constable, 1897.

Poems. London: Elkin Matthews & John Lane, 1893.

Sister Songs: An Offering to Two Sisters. London: John Lane, 1895. Also privately printed as *Songs Wing-to-Wing.*

2. Poetry, Collections

The Lost Poems of Francis Thompson. Edited by Myrtle Pihlman Pope. Ann Arbor: University Microfilms, 1966.

The Man Has Wings: New Poems and Plays by Francis Thompson. Edited by Terence L. Connolly. Garden City: Hanover House, 1957.

Poems of Francis Thompson. Edited with notes by Terence L. Connolly. New York: Century, 1932.

The Poems of Francis Thompson. Edited by Wilfrid Meynell. Oxford Standard Authors. Oxford: Oxford University Press, 1937.

Uncollected Verses by Francis Thompson. London: privately printed by Clement Shorter, 1917.

The Works of Francis Thompson. 3 vols. Vols. 1 and 2, poetry. Edited by Wilfrid Meynell. London: Burns & Oates, 1913. Reprint (3 vols. in 1).

Francis Thompson: Poems and Essays. Edited by Wilfrid Meynell. Westminster, Md: Newman, 1947.

Youthful Verses by Francis Thompson. Preston: Privately printed by Harold Halewood, 1928.

3. Prose, First Editions

Health and Holiness. London: Burns & Oates, 1905.

The Life and Labours of St. John Baptist de la Salle. London: J. Sinkins, 1891.

St. Ignatius Loyola. Edited by John H. Pollen. London: Burns & Oates, 1909. Reprint. Dublin: Clonmore & Reynolds, 1951.

Shelley: An Essay. London: Burns & Oates, 1909.

Sir Leslie Stephen as a Biographer. London: privately printed by Clement Shorter, 1915. Includes a bibliography and chronology of Thompson.

4. Prose, Collections

The Letters of Francis Thompson. Edited by John E. Walsh. New York: Hawthorn, 1969. Collects letters written by Thompson from 1887 to his death.

Literary Criticisms by Francis Thompson. Edited by Terence L. Connolly. New York: E. P. Dutton, 1948.

The Real Robert Louis Stevenson and Other Critical Essays by Francis Thompson. Edited by Terence L. Connolly. New York: University Publishers, 1959. Includes a full bibliography of Thompson's known prose.

A Renegade Poet and Other Essays. Edited by E. J. O'Brien. Boston: Ball, 1910.

The Works of Francis Thompson. Vol. 3. (See above under Poetry, Collections.)

SECONDARY SOURCES

1. Bibliographies

Pope, Myrtle Pihlman. "A Critical Bibliography of Works by and about Francis Thompson." *Bulletin of the New York Public Library* 62 (1958): 571–76; 63 (1959), 40–49, 155–61, 195–204. Includes poetry and prose.

The Real Robert Louis Stevenson. (See above under Prose, Collections.) Complete bibliography of the known prose.

The Works of Francis Thompson. Vol. 2. (See above under Poetry, Collections.) Bibliography of the poems.

2. Biography and Criticism

Connolly, Terence L. *An Account of Books and Mss. of Francis Thompson.* Newton, Mass.: Boston College, n.d. Describes some of the holdings in the Thompson Collection at Boston College.

Danchin, Pierre. *Francis Thompson: La vie et l'oeuvre d'un poète.* Paris: Nizet, 1959. Adds useful facts to the biographical material given by Everard Meynell; extensive notes and bibliography of secondary works.

Meynell, Everard. *The Life of Francis Thompson.* London and New York: Burns & Oates; Charles Scribner's Sons, 1913. Fifth edition revised, 1926. Seminal biography written by the son of Wilfrid Meynell; reticent on potentially embarrassing subjects.

Meynell, Viola. *Francis Thompson and Wilfrid Meynell: A Memoir.* London: Hollis & Carter, 1952. Reprint. New York: E. P. Dutton, 1953. Supplements Everard Meynell's *Life* on the two men's relationship, drawing material from letters and from personal recollections, by Wilfrid Meynell's daughter.

Reid, J. C. *Francis Thompson: Man and Poet.* London: Routledge & Kegan
    Paul, 1959. Contains sometimes unduly harsh literary criticism; in-
    cludes good bibliography of secondary works.
Thomson, Paul van Kuykendall. *Francis Thompson: A Critical Biography.*
    New York: Thomas Nelson, 1961. Sympathetic study; includes good
    bibliography of secondary works.
Walsh, John E. *Strange Harp, Strange Symphony: The Life of Francis Thompson.*
    New York: Hawthorn, 1967. Makes available much new material
    gleaned from unpublished manuscripts and interviews; includes very
    full notes and prints previously unpublished verse.

Index

"Judgment in Heaven, A," 26
"July Fugitive," 67
"Kingdom of God, The," 92, 130. *See
    also* "In No Strange Land"
"Larger Hope, The," 72
"Lilium Regis," 88
"Limerick, Refined," 89
"Little Jesus." *See "Ex Ore Infantium"*
"Lost Friend, A," 77
"Love and the Child," 85
"Love Declared," 42–43, 45
Love in Dian's Lap, 12, 19–25, 40,
    41, 45, 46, 47, 48, 49, 76, 78,
    83, 84
"Love, Thou Hast Suffered," 78,
    83–84
"Lover's Progress," 109
"Love's Almsman Plaineth His Fare,"
    46–47, 48
"Love Varlets," 78, 84
"Lux in Tenebris," 58
"Madonna and Child," 88
"Making of Viola, The," 35–36
"Manus Animam Pinxit," 21
"May Burden, A," 67
"Memorat Memoria," 67–68
"Miscellaneous Odes" (*New Poems*),
    59–65
"Miscellaneous Poems" (*New Poems*),
    64, 65–68
"Miscellaneous Poems" (*Poems*), 25–32
"Mistress of Vision, The," *51–53,* 54,
    55, 68, 111
"My Lady the Tyranness," 48
"My Song's Young Virgin Date," 83
Narrow Vessel, A, 12–13, *40–46,* 49,
    78, 83, 141n29
New Poems (1897), 14, 25, *39–69,*
    96, 122, 125
"New Year's Chimes," 54
"Nightmare of the Witch-Babies,
    The," 74, 109
"Nineteenth Century, The," 93
"Nisi Dominus," 88–89
"No Singer of His Time," 90
"Nocturne," 67
"Nocturnes of My Friend," 76
"Non Pax—Expectatio," 79

"O Fair and Affluent Sabbath of My
    Muse," 92
"Ode for the Diamond Jubilee of
    Queen Victoria," 93
"Ode to the English Martyrs," 94,
    140n2
"Ode to the Setting Sun," 10, *17–18,*
    52, 59, 60, 68, 91, 94, 101, 130
"Of My Friend," 141n21
"Of My Friend's Aura," 80
"Of Nature: Laud and Plaint," 87
"On a Reviewer, Calling My Poetry
    'Ambitious,' " 89
"On the Anniversary of Rossetti's
    Death," 79
"Orient Ode," 53, 56, 59
"Owl, The," 74–75, 109
"Passion of Mary, The," 9, 17, 25,
    95, 96
"Peace," 93–94
"Penelope," 43–44
"Perfect Woman, The," 134n7
Poems (1893), 12, 14, 17, *19–37,* 49,
    50, 58
"Poems on Children," 33–37
"Poet Jester, The," 89
"Poetic Sequence, A," 78, 80–81, 82
"Poet's Testament, A," 91
"Poppy, The," 33–35
"Question, A," 67
"Retrospect," 54–55
"Sad Semele," 79
"Scala Jacobi Portaque Eburnea," 22
"Schoolmaster for God, The," 89
Sight and Insight, 49–59, 61, 102
"Sing, Bird, Sing," 87
Sister Songs (1895), 11, 14, *37–38,*
    39, 58, 114
"So Now, Give O'er," 82
"Solemn Voice, The," 77
"Song of the Hours," 73, 80, 82
Songs Wing-to-Wing, 136n24
"Stella Matutinis Humanis," 85
"This Vessel Man," 82
"To a Poet Breaking Silence," 20
"To a Poet's Sitter," 23–24
"To a Snow-Flake," 66–67
"To a Wind," 77

DATE DUE

GAYLORD			PRINTED IN U.S.A.